Public Education
and the Imagination-Intellect

Cultural Critique

Norm Denzin
General Editor

Vol. 5

PETER LANG
New York • Washington, D.C./Baltimore • Bern
Frankfurt am Main • Berlin • Brussels • Vienna • Oxford

Mary E. Weems

Public Education
and the Imagination-Intellect

I Speak from the Wound in My Mouth

PETER LANG
New York • Washington, D.C./Baltimore • Bern
Frankfurt am Main • Berlin • Brussels • Vienna • Oxford

Library of Congress Cataloging-in-Publication Data

Weems, Mary E.
Public education and the imagination-intellect:
I speak from the wound in my mouth / Mary E. Weems.
p. cm. — (Cultural critique; v. 5)
Includes bibliographical references.
1. Critical pedagogy—United States. 2. Aesthetics—Study
and teaching—United States. 3. United States—Race
relations—Philosophy. I. Title. II. Series.
LC196.5.U6 W44   370.11′5—dc21   2002016252
ISBN 0-8204-5828-7
ISSN 1530-9568

Die Deutsche Bibliothek-CIP-Einheitsaufnahme

Weems, Mary E.:
Public education and the imagination-intellect:
I speak from the wound in my mouth / Mary E. Weems.
–New York; Washington, D.C./Baltimore; Bern;
Frankfurt am Main; Berlin; Brussels; Vienna; Oxford: Lang.
(Cultural critique; Vol. 5)
ISBN 0-8204-5828-7

Cover design by Joni Holst
Cover artwork by Willie Bonner
Author photo by Jim Lang

The paper in this book meets the guidelines for permanence and durability
of the Committee on Production Guidelines for Book Longevity
of the Council of Library Resources.

© 2003 Peter Lang Publishing, Inc., New York
275 Seventh Avenue, 28th Floor, New York, NY 10001
www.peterlangusa.com

Printed in the United States of America

This book is dedicated to my daughter, Michelle Elise Weems, my sister-friend-and-colleague Carolyne J. White, my sistah-friend-homey Carien Williams, Mon Amie, and Eazy, with love.

To my granny, the late Mary Isabel Lacy, and to the late African American, lesbian, feminist, warrior poet Audre Lorde.

CONTENTS

ACKNOWLEDGMENTS

I respectfully acknowledge the following people:

Ralph Page, Norm Denzin, Kal Alston, Carolyne J. White, Violet J. Harris, Cameron McCarthy, Chris Myers, Joe Kincheloe, Shirley Steinberg, Michael Elavsky, Carien Williams, and G. Mark Abrahms—this work would not have been completed without their care, concern, and support.

James Anderson, for believing in me, Clarence Shelley for being the other light in the room, Honoreé Fanon Jeffers, Gina Tabasso, and Rashid Robinson, for their feedback on I.D. PAPERS, Guadalupe Martinez and Christina Misa, for always being there for me.

Grateful acknowledgment to the following publications, where some of my work originally appeared:

Needles & Pins, Not Hatred, Inspiration. *Xcp: Cross-Cultural Poetics.*

Mirage, Death Should not Be Embarrassed, Circus. Excerpted from: My Tuesdays with Morrie. *Cultural Studies: Critical Methodologies.*

Windows. *Qualitative Inquiry.*

Tampon Class. *Calyx: A Journal of Art & Literature by Women.*

Mixup. *White.* Wick Chapbook Series. Kent State University Press.

Thank you.

EDITOR'S PREFACE

Mary Weems is a teacher, a performer, a poet, a dramatist, a theorist of the imagination intellect, an ethnographer, a critic of race relations in America's schools. Mary Weems understands public education from the inside out. As a student, an African American, a woman, an artist, and a scholar she has experienced the crushing and hurtful wound of being silenced in an educational institution. Thus her title, she speaks from the wound in her mouth.

A child of the inner cities, Mary Weems has taught and performed her poetry in alternative urban schools. Drawing on the work of John Dewey and Maxine Greene, Weems has a vision for American schools; it involves the critical, artistic imagination intellect. Dewey located lived artistic experience at the center of his educational project. Maxine Greene extends Dewey. She too locates art and artistic experiences in the lived world of students. Greene stresses the value of multicultural texts in the schooling experience, in the formation of an artistic imagination.

Weems, after Greene and Dewey, emphasizes the importance of aesthetic appreciation and aesthetic expression in K-12 public school classrooms. These activities release the imagination intellect. They create the space for schooling that builds on the unique experiences of each child. These activities lay the foundations for radical social change, for change, to quote Weems, which "envisions a democracy founded in a social justice that is 'not yet.'"

Weems believes that is time to think through the practical, progressive politics of a performative cultural studies: a critical emancipatory discourse connecting theory, praxis, ethics, and knowledge. She asks how the performance-based human disciplines can contribute to radical social change, to economic justice and a cultural politics which extends "the principles of a radical democracy to all aspects of society" (Giroux, 2000a, pp. x, 25; Giroux, 2001; 2000b; also Diawara 1996, p. 305; Kincheloe and McLaren, 2000, p. 282).

In Weems's model there are five core areas or dimensions to the critical imagination intellect. Each dimension involves a student developing a set of critical, interpretive skills and practices.

The first skill is **aesthetic appreciation.** Schooling should teach students how to value intercultural art produced by heterosexual, feminist, and gay artists. The second dimension involves **oral expression,** helping students become improvisational storytellers. The third practice applies to **written expression,** teaching children how to write poetry, fiction and plays. The fourth area speaks to **performance skills,** giving children the confidence and self-esteem they need so they can feel comfortable performing and communicating their own artistic work. Fifth, the imagination intellect focuses on **social consciousness.** Weems feels that children need to learn an intercultural history. This history gives them an awareness of their social position in society. It enables them to honor diversity and to put social justice, including true participatory democracy, at the forefront of their lives.

In Weems's ideal school the curriculum includes classes titled "Creativity Class," "Exercise and Meditation," "Math and Us," "History Is About All of Us," "Becoming a Citizen of the World." Classes are team taught and non-competitive. Parents are free to visit the school throughout the day. Classrooms are without walls. The school fosters a nurturing environment of love, respect, and reciprocal learning and sharing. There are no grades in the traditional sense. Instead, each eight-week period is marked by student performances. There are three performance categories: rhetorical debate, scientific discovery, and creative performances. Oral examinations and/or artistic performances determine promotion to the next grade level.

Weems observes that five-year-old children enter the public school classroom with creative, vibrant, playful imagination-intellects, full of questions and excited about learning. In the ensuing years they lose this imagination-intellect; they experience mis-education. They pass through the public school classrooms without the possibility of developing socially conscious imagination-intellects. Like Greene and Dewey, Mary Weems is a utopian thinker. She believes that schools can be different. For this to happen there must be a moral commitment to a set of pedagogical practices that foster the imagination-intellect, connecting it to the creative artistic imagination.

Weems's project is embedded in a rich and deep literature. She draws from the work of such radical multicultural educational theorists as Paulo Freire, Cameron McCarthy, Joe Kincheloe, Peter McLaren, Shirley Steinberg, and Henry Giroux, theorists of a practical, political pedagogy, a pedagogy that would make schools a place where children, teachers, parents, and administrators have respectful, caring, loving, empowering experiences.

In the pages of this wonderfully powerful and lyrical book she brings her version of the imagination-intellect alive. Her autoethnographic, sacred performance text is a radical, interpretive act. In her words "it is an exemplar of, and an argument for the critical, imagination-intellect." Weems wants this book to inspire and challenge educators, teachers, and students to use the language arts as their weapon of choice in our nation's classrooms. She wants to encourage teachers, students, parents, and others to become activists in the political struggle surrounding educational reform. Education is the key to developing a truly unbiased, liberated society.

Teacher education programs must address personal and institutional racism. This is especially critical, as the population of non-white students increases, and the public school teaching population "gets whiter and whiter." Weems in no way intends to blame or group all white Americans together, as being racist. She merely wants them to acknowledge the role of the powerful in controlling the powerless.

She issues a four-fold call. She asks all "responsible traitors" to step forward. She asks that they acknowledge that their whiteness is both a privilege and a social construct. She challenges white educators to struggle against their prejudices. She asks them to adopt an activist position, to challenge injustice while engaging in practices that facilitate the education and empowerment of Native Americans, African Americans, Latino/a Americans and Asian Americans.

Weems stands on the shoulders of Toni Morrison, Rita Dove, Ntozake Shange, Anna Deveare Smith, June Jordan, Audre Lorde, Pearl S. Cleague, and Wanda Coleman. These artist-scholar African American poets and writers use their work as sites of protest. Like these activists, Weems reaches back to re-member and re-connect with her ancestors who were denied the power of education.

Weems's book also extends the project of the Harlem Renaissance writers, including Zora Neale Hurston, Georgia Douglas Johnson, Alice Dunbar-Nelson, Langston Hughes, Claude McKay, and Richard Wright. As she observes, her work also emerges out of the Black Arts movement of the 1960s, and the writings of such artist-activist-scholars as Amiri Baraka (Leroi Jones), Malcolm X, Jane Cortez, Sonia Sanchez, Nikki Giovanni, and Maya Angelou.

Following critical pedagogy theorists Giroux, McLaren, Kincheloe, and Steinberg, Weems wants her work to challenge the racist foundations of urban education. She seeks to inspire teachers, students, and parents to work within "a liberatory pedagogical framework" (Kincheloe and McLaren, 2000, p. 280). As an educator, creative writer, and performer, Weems expands the notion of critical pedagogy by going beyond theory, and putting it into praxis, by "responding to institutionalized racism with original performance texts" which, like those of Anna Deveare Smith, she brings to life for an audience.

The opening and closing theoretical chapters of Weems's book focus on the imagination-intellect. Chapters Two and Three are autoethnographic plays. *Dirt*, is inspired by Shange's play, *For Colored Girls Who Have Committed Suicide When the Rainbow Is Enuf. Graffiti This! No Rembrant in the Hood* is based on a negative aesthetic experience Weems had in graduate school. Chapter Four, *ID Papers*, is a collection of poems, meant, like all poetry, to be read aloud.

Poetry is the most evocative of literary genres, the genre most open to multiple interpretations, co-ownership, and co-performance. In her poetry, which she likens to the blues, Weems invites each reader to become a co-performer with her, to move from where she has come (*Dirt*) to where she is going as an activist artist educator. In her poems she "floats between history, memory, and myth." Indeed, each chapter in her book is a blues statement, birthed, she tells us, "from my spirit adept at playing the blues while struggling for the jazz of freedom on a troubled American landscape."

In her recent study of the female blues singers, Ma Rainey, Bessie Smith, and Billie Holiday, Angela Davis (1998) observes that within AfricanAmerican culture, the "blues marked the advent of a popular culture of performance, with the borders of performer and audience becoming increasing differentiated... this... mode of presenting popular music crystallized into a performance culture that has had an enduring influence on African-American music" (p. 5).

In her performance texts, Weems follows Ma Rainey, Bessie Smith, and Billie Holiday. In their performances these blues singers presented a set of black feminist understandings concerning class, race, gender, violence, sexuality, marriage, men, and intimacy. Weems's work is part of this blues tradition. It is deeply entrenched in an indigenous, class conscious, black feminism. Close your eyes and listen to Weems as she sings with the female blues singers. Together, Weems, Ma Rainey, Bessie, and Billie do the "Good News Blues" (Jordan, 1998, pp. 182–200) you can feel it in your bones,

 I been lost
 but
 I been found

I am bound
—for Billie's land (Jordan, 1998, p. 199).

The voices of these blues poets create performance spaces for black women and their children, spaces to sing and live the blues; black voices talking and doing black culture; a new black planet; a public, critical black performance art, the critical imagination-intellect at work.

The blues are improvised songs of pain, sorrow. and hope, sung from the heart. Rainey, Smith, and Holiday sang in ways that went beyond the written text. They turned the blues into a living art form, a form that would, with Holiday, move into the spaces of jazz. And jazz, like the blues, is also an improvisational, not a static art form. Bill Evans, the great be-bop pianist put it this way, "Jazz is not a what... it is a how. If it were a what, it would be static, never growing. The how is that the music comes from the moment, it is spontaneous, it exists at the time it is created" (Evans, quoted in Lee, 1996, p. 426). The improvised co-performance text, like a jazz solo, like Billie Holiday doing the blues, is a spontaneous production; it lives in the moment of creation.

This is what Mary Weems's art does. It lives in the moment of creation. In that moment it fits Emily Dickinson's famed description of what good poetry should do, that is, "if you feel that the top of your head has been taken off, the poem is good." This is how I feel when Mary reads her poetry. She turns my world around, takes off the top of my head, and makes me see differently. She moves me to action. I am certain she will do the same for you.

At the beginning of the twenty-first century, there is a pressing demand to show how the practices of critical, interpretive qualitative research can help change the world in positive ways. It is necessary to examine new ways of making the practices of critical qualitative inquiry central to the workings of a free democratic society. Critical scholars must ask how the discourses of qualitative research can be used to help create and imagine a free democratic society. Such a society is one that dares to confront and challenge the central problem of 20th-century America; namely what W. E. B. Du Bois (1903) called the problem of the color line.

Interpretive work must be focused around a clear set of moral and political goals. Within this moral framework the challenge to interpretive scholars of race, education, and society is clear. How can we use our interpretive work to empower those students of color who have been victims of racial injustice and racial oppression? Mary Weems's bold, innovative book is a model for the rest of us. We owe Mary a great debt. She tells us how to make these differences happen.

— Norman K. Denzin
Series Editor

It is our pleasure as series editors to welcome Mary Weems to the Cultural Critique series. When Norm Denzin sent us this book in its manuscript form, I (Joe) opened it, started reading, and literally could not put it down. I was captivated by Mary's unique use of the language, her ability to make her own and other experiences come alive. I found myself pondering particular sentences, phrases, and metaphors in ways not common to the reading of academic books. Is this an academic book? Most definitely. Is it unique? Absolutely. We hope that Mary's book will exert as profound effect on the field as it did as we read the manuscript. Such influence will certainly make academia a more interesting venue. It is rare that such a volume comes along. It is unusual that series editors have a chance to watch a book of this caliber move through the publishing process. We want to thank Norm for having the educated, aesthetic eye to recognize the genius of this work. We also, of course, want to thank Mary for publishing in our series. We are confident that this is just the first of a number of profound creations from Dr. Weems. As always we appreciate the publishing vision of Chris Myers—a perspective that welcomes framebreaking contributions like this.

—Joe L. Kincheloe
CUNY Graduate Center/Brooklyn College
—Shirley R. Steinberg
Montclair State University

NOTES:

Davis, Angela Y. 1998. *Blues Legacies and Black Feminism*. New York: Pantheon.

Diawara, Mantha. 1996. "Black Studies, Cultural Studies: Performative Acts." Pp. 300–306 in John Storey (Ed.), *What Is Cultural Studies*. London: Arnold.

Du Bois, W. E. B. 1903. *The Souls of Black Folk: Essays and Sketches*. New York: Fawcett. (Reprinted, 1989, New York: Bantam.)

Giroux, Henry. 2001.Cultural Studies as Performative Politics." *Cultural Studies—Critical Methodologies*. 1: 5–23.

Giroux, Henry. 2000a. *Impure Acts: The Practical Politics of Cultural Studies.* New York: Routledge.

Giroux, Henry. 2000b. *Stealing Innocence: Corporate Culture's War on Children.* New York: Palgrave.

Jordan, June. 1998. *Affirmative Acts.* New York: Doubleday.

Kincheloe, Joe L. and Peter McLaren. 2000. "Rethinking Critical Theory and Qualitative Research." Pp. 279–314 in N. K. Denzin and Y. S. Lincoln (Eds.). *Handbook of Qualitative Research*, 2/e. Thousand Oaks: Sage.

Lee, Gene. 1996. "The Poet: Bill Evans." Pp. 419–444 in Robert Gottlieb (Ed.), *Reading Jazz: A Gathering of Autobiography, Reportage, and Criticism from 1919 to Now.* New York: Pantheon.

PREFACE

This auto/ethnographic, sacred performance text is a radical, interpretive, political act. It is an exemplar of, and an argument for, what I am calling critical, imagination-intellectual development as a primary goal in K-12 public schools. It's philosophically centered in John Dewey's aesthetic experience, and Maxine Greene's aesthetic appreciation and expression, and Norman K. Denzin's seventh moment. I want this work to inspire other educators, students, and teachers to use the arts, particularly the language arts, as what Gordon Parks calls their "choice of weapon." While urban education reform is my central focus, the possibilities for a population armed with astute, critical, imagination-intellects for using performance texts as political acts extend beyond this parameter to all other social institutions and issues.

I want this work to push others to join artist-scholars like Toni Morrison, Ntozake Shange, Anna Deveare Smith, Audre Lorde, Pearl S. Cleague, Nikki Giovanni, and Wanda Coleman, who use their work as sites of protest. Like these activists, my writings reach back, re-member, and re-connect with our ancestors who were denied the power of education.

This book continues the work of the Harlem Renaissance writers including Zora Neale Hurston, Georgia Douglas Johnson, Alice Dunbar-Nelson, Langston Hughes, Claude McKay, and Richard Wright. It emerges from the power of the black arts movement of the 1960s, expressed in the writings of artist-scholars like Amiri Baraka (Leroi Jones), El Haj Malik Shabazz (Malcolm X), Nikki Giovanni, Gwendolyn Brooks, Maya Angelou, Ishmael Reed, The Last Poets, and Gil Scott Heron.

In addition to standing on the shoulders of people like the artist-scholars mentioned above, my work is linked to the contemporary critical theory/pedagogy of scholar-artists like Henry Giroux, Joe Kincheloe, and Peter McLaren. It is concerned with the "social construction of lived experience," with challenging the racist foundation of public schooling, with inspiring teachers, students, and others to work within a "liberatory pedagogical framework" (Kincheloe & McClaren, 2000, p. 280) and express their socio-political views in culturallyspecific performance texts. As an educator, creative writer, and performer, I expand notions of critical pedagogy by not only developing theory and putting it into praxis, but by responding to institutionalized racism with original performance texts, which, like Anna Deveare Smith, I bring to life for an audience.

I want to encourage teachers, students, parents, and others to become activists in the political struggle for systemic, urban education reform because this is where many students are being mis- and under-educated. Education is essential to developing an activist, political stance. It is essential to establishing a true, participatory democracy, and ultimately an unbiased, liberated society.

At the university level teacher education programs must address racism, institutionalized racism, cultural relevancy, and language tolerance to better prepare their teachers to teach in diverse, and often re-segregated urban environments. This is particularly critical as the population of non-whites increases, and the public school teaching population gets whiter and whiter.

Throughout this book I will use the terms racist, eurocentrism, white, and America to refer to a specific group of Americans who orchestrated the genocide of Native Americans, sexism, slavery, racism, and the founding of common schools. I in no way intend to group all white Americans together or to discount the contributions and sacrifices thousands have made in the name of freedom, justice, equity, and urban education reform. My purpose is not to blame, but rather to acknowledge the role of the powerful in controlling and exploiting the power-less, and to call for more white folks who Lisa Heldke (1998, p. 94) defines as "responsible traitors" to step forward. First, white folks should acknowledge whiteness as a social construct, and their position as privileged individuals. Second, they should develop an awareness of and struggle against their prejudices toward non-whites. Third, responsible white traitors should adopt an activist position by challenging injustice, and by facilitating educational, employment, publication, and other empowering possibilities for Native Americans, African Americans, Latino/a Americans, and Asian Americans.

Each chapter of this book is a blues statement birthed from my spirit adept at playing the blues while struggling for the jazz of freedom on a troubled American landscape.

Two chapters frame this text. "Utopia: Imagination-Intellect as a Pedagogical Focus" defines the imagination-intellectual construct. It discusses some of the artist-scholars, and scholar-artists including John Dewey, Maxine Greene, bell hooks, W.E.B. DuBois, Paulo Freire, and Norman K. Denzin, whose work inform this theory. It explains why critical, imagination-intellectual expansion should be a primary goal of public schools. It discusses the importance of facilitating this development through aesthetic appreciation, expression, and experiences filtered through each student's culturally specific lens.

"Dirt" is an auto/ethnographic play, inspired by Ntozaka Shange's play *For Colored Girls Who Have Committed Suicide When the Rainbow Is Enuf.* I explore issues of identity, racism, internalized racism, institutionalized racism, sexism, and social justice. I re-memory and re-interpret my life's journey to discover the powerful, African American woman I am still becoming. Dirt is the metaphor and the trope that weaves the piece together in a play that can be shared and re-interpreted by a reader/audience concerned with issues of race, sex, and identity.

The play may be engaged as one of Dewey's aesthetic experiences, a way of empathizing with the lived experience of one African American woman, and reaching an epiphany or some new understanding. It is as an exemplar of aesthetic appreciation as the reader/audience reads, and/or watches the play performed and recognizes it as the artistic creation of a flawed, human being. Excerpts from *Dirt,* or a character, or theme can inspire others to create new work, as Shange's play was the catalyst for it.

"Graffiti This! No Rembrandt in the Hood" is a play that exists because of a negative aesthetic experience I had in a graduate level aesthetics and the curriculum course where I was the lone African American voice. It is a creative reconstruction; an auto/ethnographic response to institutionalized racism in a teacher education course. It challenges privileged eurocentric notions of art. The play addresses the need for dialogue around issues of race, cultural relevancy, language tolerance, empathy, and compassion, in all teacher education courses. "Graffiti This!" may be used in the same manner as "Dirt," and would be a powerful addition to all teacher education curricula as a way of framing a discussion around institutionalized racism and the other areas noted above as missing in many of these programs.

"I.D. Papers" is a collection of poems inspired by a poem by Kimiko Hahn titled "Cruising Barthes." The three sections: (1) I.D. Papers, (2) Souvenirs, and (3) Windows further explore the issues addressed in the two plays. By using poetry, the genre most open to multiple interpretations, co-ownership, and co-performance, it moves me from where I've come from ("Dirt"), where I've been ("Graffiti This! No Rembrandt in the Hood"), to where I'm going as an activist artist educator, and qualitative researcher, which is further away from traditional scholarship, and closer to radical, experimental performance texts as my choice of weapon. In these poems I float between history, memory, and myth; my past, present, and future are all *now*.

"Nurturing the Imagination–Intellect" is a scholarly bookend. The second framing chapter, it describes ways to nurture socially conscious, imagination-intellectual development in public school classrooms.

NOTES:

Heldke, Lisa. 1998. "On Being a Responsible Traitor A Primer." in Bat-Ami Bar On and Ann Ferguson (Eds.), *Daring to be Good: Essays in Feminist Ethico-Politics.* New York: Routledge.

Kincheloe, Joe L., and Peter McLaren. 2000. "Rethinking Critical Theory and Qualitative Research." Pp. 279–314 in N.K. Denzin and Y.S. Lincoln (Eds.), *Handbook of Qualitative Research, 2/e.* Thousand Oaks: Sage.

CHAPTER ONE
UTOPIA: CRITICAL IMAGINATION—
INTELLECT AS A PEDAGOGICAL FOCUS

Imagination: The formation of a mental image or concept of that which is not real or present. A mental image or idea. The ability or tendency to form such mental images or concepts. The ability to deal creatively with reality.

Intellect: The ability to learn and reason as distinguished from the ability to feel or will; capacity for knowledge and understanding. The ability to think abstractly or profoundly. A person of great intellectual ability. The intellectual members of a group.
(*American Heritage Dictionary*)

Like the human heart and its arteries, the imagination and intellect are inextricably linked; they develop simultaneously and, I suggest, one is not possible without the other. Paulo Freire (1985, p. 70) asserts that what distinguishes human labor (he uses an architect as an example) from the work of bees is our ability to begin by building an idea in our imagination.

I posit that like Freire's architect all ideas are first imagined, then intellectually developed in an interconnected process which mirrors the blood's circulation through the body, and like blood, this connection is essential to what Hofstader describes as the intellectual-life (1962).

It is a mistake to separate imagination, intellect, will, and emotion. We learn with our whole mind. New ideas and reflection incorporate imagination, reason, logic, and the passion that drives us to pursue research, to ask questions, and to take risks. It is not possible to formulate an idea without reflection, or to develop an idea without imagination. The creation of new knowledge often consumes a lifetime, and the discipline, dedication, and tenacity for imagination-intellectual pursuits could not occur without a sustained level of emotion.

Q: When an artist writes a scholarly paper does she cease being an artist? When a scholar creates a poem does she cease being a scholar?

I say no. My conceptualization of the imagination-intellect stems first from asking the above question after re-seeing the work of other artist-scholars and scholar-artists within the context of my own work. Second, my theory is prompted by my experience as a student whose urban public education mirrored the *banking education* Paulo Freire (1985) defined as teachers (bankers depositing information into empty students. Third, it's been developed during my eight years of field experience as an artist educator teaching oral-literate performance-based, creative writing workshops.

John Dewey posits that "lived experience" and "the arts" are at the center of education. And an aesthetic experience is a barometer for evaluating artistic creations via each individual's interaction with the work. For Dewey, reaching an epiphany or new understanding about yourself and/or the world is a crucial epistemological element. This auto/ethnographic (see: Denzin, 1997b, 1999; White, 1995; White et al., 1996; White et al., 1998; Beach et al., 1999; Noblitt, 1999; Roberts, 1993) work flows from my own lived experience as an artist-scholar. It includes both negative and positive aesthetic experiences, and embraces these tenets of Dewey's philosophy.

Maxine Greene's work privileges multicultural texts as a way of learning more about unfamiliar cultures. She emphasizes the importance of aesthetic appreciation and aesthetic expression in the K-12 public school experience. At the heart of Greene's notion of aesthetic appreciation is the necessity of teaching students to view artistic creations first as the work of human beings. This means facilitating their understanding that art does not belong on an unreachable pedestal, but rather in the lived world where students can learn how to enjoy and evaluate it.

Aesthetic expression for Greene means that all public school students should have an opportunity, once they've learned to appreciate the art of others, to create their own. Greene is not using an essentialized notion of aesthetics, but rather an aesthetics rooted in the culture, race, ethnicity, sexual orientation, and/or religion of the individual/group.

Like me, she believes that aesthetic appreciation and expression should be at the heart of all educative endeavors as they "release the imagination" of students. This release coupled with guidance from teachers committed to liberation and equity helps them envision a democracy founded in a social justice that is "not yet."

The philosophical approach to teaching as an art centered around creating a loving, culturally relevant communal where the language, customs, and historical backgrounds, of all students are respected, welcomed, and viewed as a valuable aspect of each student's knowledge base (See: Ladson-Billings, 1994; Scheurich, 1998; Greene, 1995) is an integral part of imagination-intellectual growth.

This is crucial because students from all ethnic and cultural backgrounds need strong, socially conscious imagination-intellects and a safe, loving learning environment. But it is the oppressed, disempowered peoples of color who need the positive reinforcement of the parallel value of their cultures in the face of racism and eurocentrism.

American ambivalence toward intellectuals and a narrow de facto definition of intellect prohibits the acknowledgement of artists as intellectuals and the recognition of art as intellectual property. Conversely, while at their best intellectuals including scientists, mathematicians, philosophers, engineers, and teachers create new knowledge or complete the development of the "formation of a mental image or concept of that which is not real or present"; they are rarely identified as artists.

How has the lack of focus on the imagination-intellect contributed to the dysfunctional state of public education? How have we moved from the quasi-visionary view Maxine Greene described (1965, p. 3) when discussing the foundation of public schooling in the early nineteenth century? This was a time when the powerful purportedly believed that not only would schools teach assimilation, but they would also equip young people for the responsibilities of freedom. How have we moved to a banking educational system where one of the main questions students ask is "Will it be on the test?" (Larabee, 1997, p. 68). Implicit in this question is the idea that anything outside exam parameters is not required knowledge, and therefore "not worth learning" (Larabee, 1997, p. 68).

Teaching students to *think* by facilitating imagination-intellectual development, by integrating aesthetic appreciation, oral expression, written expression, and performance into the curriculum should be the primary goal of education. That focus will create an increasingly imagination-intellectually astute student population well-equipped to love the pursuit of knowledge, to question, to criticize, to affect positive social change.

I embrace Denzin's seventh moment (Denzin and Lincoln, 2000, p. 1048). It continues a liberation movement where the center shifts with each new, previously silenced voice. He notes that like blues music, qualitative research is filled with breaks and ruptures rather than smooth evolution, and theories move in and out of popularity. As a qualitative researcher, I share Denzin's vision and conviction that the ideas, needs, and dreams of the othered is where a moral discourse that moves us closer to where a true participatory democracy begins.

As for how the moral imagination-intellect should be developed, this is a crucial issue that must be addressed in the public school classroom lest we foster aesthetically appreciative oppressors, serial killers, or Ellsworth Tooheys' (see: Ayn Rand's *Fountainhead*). But as an African American woman, I am constantly slipping on the stones of marginalization, mis-education in public schools filled with the moral rhetoric delineated in the Pledge of Allegiance, incomplete and downright wrong history and English books, and lunch time prayer.

I believe in the Golden Rule. Students have many other positive and negative environments that help shape their moral fiber. If public school classrooms could communicate the importance of treating others the way they want to be treated, of developing the kind of empathy Greene encourages within the context of diversity and difference, this would be a step in a powerful social direction.

What would happen if the millions of dollars channeled into testing and teaching students strategies for passing proficiency exams were redirected toward facilitating the development of the imagination-intellect from grades K-12?

Some may argue that all human beings are not capable of imagination-intellectual development. Yet, barring some physical and intellectually debilitating abnormality of the brain, I agree with artist-scholars and scholar-artists like Paulo Freire and bell hooks who purport that learning and the creation of knowledge IS for and within the grasp of the masses. hooks's text *Teaching to Transgress* (1994, p. 2) opens with a quote by Paulo Freire (1985, p. xxiii) who believed that all human beings are interpretive-intellectuals constantly participating in the world. In the book hooks cites her public school experience in the South as one of being nurtured by black teachers. She was encouraged to develop a love of learning, and to view education as freedom, as essential to an ongoing political struggle.

How many imagination-intellectual lives, how many future artists-scholars, and scholar-artists have been lost in public schools due to chronic boredom and systematic stagnation?

"Feeling predicts intelligence."
(Baraka, 1995, p. 132).

Utopia

The school is built on the round. Straight rows, silence, and conformity are banned and when you walk in the round door two signs greet you: "Education is freedom" and "We are thinkers." A sound system plays music selected from all of the different cultures in America. The walls are covered with the art of people from all over the world. There is a video room, where art films on dance, sculpture, print making, photography, painting, and other aesthetic disciplines are shown. There is a game room filled with learning games for student time-outs. Teachers, happy to be there, mirror the faces of their students. They are from all over the world, possess vibrant imagination-intellects, and are there to facilitate learning how to learn, while they learn from each student. Five areas are at the core of imagination-intellectual development:

1. Aesthetic appreciation: Based on Maxine Greene's theory that all artistic expression must first be experienced as the creation of human beings. I interpret this to mean that students need to view art, listen to music, attend dance programs, read and discuss poems, plays, short stories, and novels beginning in kindergarten. Teachers need to facilitate open discussions that help the students articulate an appreciation for an intercultural selection of art by heterosexual, feminist, and gay artists helping students develop a socially unbiased creative-critical eye.

2. Oral expression: Assisting students in becoming personally engaged with language through *improvisational* storytelling, rapping, flowing, hip hop, improvisational skits, debate, and public speaking. These unrehearsed expressions could also be responses to the artistic creations of others. Becoming an effective oral performer and/or presenter boosts student self-esteem while helping them develop a valuable ability. It is general knowledge that many people are more afraid of speaking in front of an audience than they are of dying.

3. Written expression: Encouraging students to explore language through the creation of poetry, short fiction, plays, reflecting their own lived experience, and by responding as readers to the creative work of an intercultural selection of published authors.

4. Performance: Increasing student self-esteem, and their ability to communicate effectively through the memorization and dramatic presentation of original work, the work of published authors, and/or a hybrid mix where they take the work of a published author and incorporate their own work. This area differs from #2 because improvisational oral expression occurs in the moment, while a polished performance takes time to prepare, and should be facilitated by someone with acting and/or performance poetry skills.

5. Social consciousness: Students need to learn an intercultural history, an awareness of their social position in society enabling them to honor diversity, and to put social justice including the importance of a true participatory democracy at the forefront. A creative-critical, social consciousness shapes an imagination-intellect capable of envisioning, and

actively working toward a better, more humane world.

The principal stands just inside the door each morning. He greets each student by name. There are no bells to ring to remind a student to get to class, that class has started, or that the day's ended. Days flow in activities designed to promote imagination-intellectual development, and when it's time to switch classes the teachers let the students know.

The school covers grades K-12 and the curriculum includes classes titled "Creativity Class Where We Get to Make Up Stuff," "Exercise and Meditation to Keep Our Minds and Bodies Healthy," "Math and Us," "History Is About All of Us," "Eastern and Western Philosophers" and "Becoming a Citizen of the World." Each class is team taught because the teachers, parents, and administrators believe that two heads are better than one in terms of assessing the best non-competitive way to encourage students to do their best thinking. All cultures have parallel value and the language, customs, and histories of each are given class time, and students are encouraged to read beyond classroom texts, by their parents, teachers, and by visits to the school's well-stocked library. Parents are free to visit the school throughout the day. Some come to observe, some come to share their unique talents with the students and teachers, some share their real-life narratives.

Classrooms are without walls and furnished with large, round learning tables, and different shapes and textures of chairs, and talking and movement while learning is encouraged—never punished.

Attendance fluctuates between 95% and 100% because the school has a nurturing environment of love, mutual respect, reciprocal learning, and sharing, and everyone looks forward to school each day. There are no grades in the traditional sense. Instead, each eight-week period is marked by student performances which are attended by teachers, administrators, parents, and the community-at-large. There are three categories: Rhetorical Debate, Scientific Discovery, and Creative Performances grounded in literature, history, math, and any of the physical sciences.

Each day students are encouraged to ask questions and critique the information shared by their teachers—to develop new ideas about the subject matter they're studying, and to both appreciate the art of others and to create art themselves. Oral and written expression is part of each teacher's daily lesson plan and prolonged silence by any student is considered a cause for alarm. Teacher-parent-student conferences are arranged to determine what may be done to help the student participate. Discipline problems are addressed in this same manner, and the focus is on what is best for the student—*not* punishment.

At the end of each semester, promotion to the next grade level is determined by oral examinations and/or artistic performances. Questions are developed by teachers and students in higher grade levels designed to gauge how much the student has learned how to learn. Throughout the school year, kudos is given for the performance of original work, formulating and developing an idea, or asking a profound question.

At various intervals, an observer might see older students reading to younger students, two kindergartners debating a question, a group of students working on a math problem, or students and teachers involved in learning-based play. Everyone connected with the school believes that the imagination and intellect are inseparable and that learning how to learn is the most important talent each student needs for a life filled with the love of learning, the creation of new knowledge, and the pursuit of social justice.

The above attempt to describe my version of a utopian public school is admittedly flawed and naive in terms of its exclusion of the complex external political forces that have shaped public education from its inception. But it may be a lot closer to the vision of artist-scholars like Maxine Greene than the majority of public school classrooms today. According to Greene (1995, p. 3) our ability to empathize is linked to our capacity to imagine it is what allows us to envision alternative realities.

To facilitate this development, students need the opportunity to explore their own creativity through play, oral storytelling, the creative writing and performance of poems, stories, and plays, rhetorical debate, interrogation, and critique. To the extent that this exploration occurs in a public school setting it seems counter-productive to create the social mobility-based atmosphere of individual competition, especially in a diverse cultural climate where collectivism or group interaction, not individualism, may be more in keeping with the cultural background of many of the students.

In her text *Dreamkeepers* Gloria Ladson-Billings (1994, p. 12) assesses her own public school experience making a distinction between elementary and middle school by noting that her elementary school teachers encouraged achievement, but did not create competitiveness among students by highlighting her academic abilities. Once Ladson-Billings entered middle school this changed. She encountered white students accustomed to an individualistic, unfair, competitive I-got-mine-you-get-yours mentality.

When children enter the public school classroom at five years old, they possess vibrant, playful imagination-intellects; they are full of questions, and are excited about learning. What happens in the ensuing years as they sit in classrooms where the physical space is a Puritan leftover with its straight rows, uncomfortable chairs and too small desks, being fed information like pabulum, forced to be silent until called upon?

What is the affect on their imagination-intellects of a focus on analysis and exposition before they've had an opportunity to realize their own creative abilities? What would an argument against the imagination-intellect sound like? Freire (1985, p. 102) sheds light when he suggests that those of us who are not members of the dominant group would be naive to think the powerful would develop an educational system designed to help us realize our socio-economic position, to begin to struggle en masse for justice

Is it possible as Freire seems to imply that one of the political arguments against the imagination-intellect would be that it would encourage the freedom of thought which would allow *othered* cultures to critically assess the system of social injustice they live under and begin to struggle for positive social change? A person who possesses an imagination-intellectually astute mind is free in a way that has little to do with socio-economic position or physical location.

The plight of journalist, activist, Move member, Mumia Abu-Jamal who's been on death row for 17 years spending 23 hours a day in a space the size of a small bathroom, yet continues to create, and speak out serves as an example. Richard Wright's daughter, Julia Wright, writes in her preface to Abu-Jamal's book *Death Blossoms* (1997, p. xvii–xviii) that his work is a story of escape from prison into the unending freedom of a mind committed to the revolution for social justice.

At their best, all teachers, principals, and administrators committed to social justice, and to teaching as an art, should be the dreamkeepers Ladson-Billings highlights in her book acting as artist-scholars, and teacher-learners in landscapes designed to teach students how to learn. As Native American Sherman Alexie (1993, pp. 152–153) so poignantly articulates, "Imagination is the politics of dreams."

To echo the late poet Langston Hughes: What has happened to the deferred dreams of the millions of children who have passed through public school classrooms mis-educated (See: Woodson, 1992) and without an opportunity to develop their, socially conscious, imagination-intellects?

The next five chapters, "Dirt," "Graffiti This! No Rembrandt in the Hood," "I.D. Papers," "Souvenirs," and "Windows," are exemplars of an astute critical, imagination-intellect. These pedagogical forms are inspired by my childhood, young adulthood, and graduate experiences. They are performance texts that may be used in English, Creative Writing, Teacher Education, Theater, and other classrooms across the curriculum to explore issues of identity, racism, institutionalized racism, internalized racism, and sexism. Performed or read silently, they prompt critical engagement, student/adult dialogue about the social issues they encompass, and constructive action, including the creation of new performance texts based on the lived experiences of the reader/audience.

CHAPTER TWO
TRANSITIONS

Sankofa: One must return to the past in order to move forward

1. Mona

She is the sound of the name
and the name. Lolling under a white
eye, a photo op, synthetic hair Barbie-Doll-Blonde,
skin the brown of question marks,
bananas that haven't made up their
mind, the Temptations without David.
Sankofa follows. She runs to the camera and
from a voice that takes her anyway.

> *what is the white man thinking his camera*
> *the end of his arm, its tight focus avoiding,*
> *his skin the color of bones on the beach*

Sankofa talks her into the dungeons where
yesterday waits in obsidian-iron-collared eyes,
her attempts to leave push her further,

> *white hands pull her head back*
> *like the trigger on a gun   strip*
> *the latest fashion from her back*
> *hot-brands her skin*

the past a womb, a wound. She is wound
around the fingers of the men, women, children
twirled like a top and cast.

She drops through a hole and lands on
the map of the Middle. All the voices
are all the voices. She hears her
name change. Others try it on
their tongues. Spirit they call her "Shola"
she walks through cane.

2. Shola

>*Every time she sees the massa*
>*she is un-fucked from behind*
>*his mouth a ditch for shit*

The plantation divides like separate arms
some hold the whip, trace his footsteps,
report the smell of freedom in the grass.
When they sing the massa takes it all,
grins in his whiskey, gives each
traitor a flag, a clean rag, and an extra
plate of food

>*"You mean I got me a nigga that can't*
>*count and whoop at the same time?*
>*You're gonna be whoopin' niggers*
>*til you die!"*

>*the woman is birth*
>*caught running free her eyes run*
>*with the whip-forced-black-hand*
>*when she dies*
>*her son is born*

some refuse to eat from the house
preferring the grass or nothing
drink water from a hole they've dug
for rage. When horror comes like
sun and moon eyes go to The hills
to be.

3. Shonga

"The snake will have whatever is in the belly
of the frog" he shouts looking up to a sky
filled with wooden cages. Each one holds a
black man looking for God in the eyes of vultures
eating their fingers, and toes. On the ground white
men take a lunch break, sweep the body
parts that fall into neat piles and feed them
to the frogs.

4. NuNu

She is the cool breeze, God's first wife.
She walks among the ghosts killing them with words.

Her son crawls to the Christian altar on his belly
looking for salvation in blue eyes. Seeing the devil
in his mother, he knows she's a heathen
and kills her when she won't repent.

This Evolution Will Not Be Televised

One million poems, and blood
paintings pressed between fingers
not leaving prints

Picasso and the brotha from another planet
passing each other on a New York street,
the brotha pullin' his coat, Picasso
opening his trench to reveal his wares
hanging from the lining like cheap,
imitation watches

Meanwhile watching the fun ghosts
smoking huge dollar bills walk
down fast streets stepping on all
the cracks

Mothers create dance in large kitchens
with wooden floors, the mistress
of the house sits in the pantry quietly
taking notes

Contrary to popular belief Claude McKay's
tombstone does not say "fuck all you mothafuckas"
and James Brown was the Godfather of soul
before time started

Starting to look around can hurt if you black
and wonder why everybody carries
copies of your work in back pockets
while your paint brushes rest in jelly jars,
you canvas shop in the backs of grocery store
parking lots days food is delivered
Basquiat and Hendrix took a long trip
all their baggage was pawned the day
after they left

George Carlin said white folks should never,
ever play the blues their job is to give the blues
to blacks

Our image, our braids, our music, our mistakes,
our asses, our rhythms are played on TV
like a long 78 album in commercial after commercial

The Colonel in plantation-dress raps and moonwalks
selling a black woman's stolen fried chicken, black kids
snap their fingers, think that's so cool, bug their mamas
for extra-crispy

This is a never-ending story, that won't be televised
but:

Baraka already wrote a poem about it
Miles played it on the way to the grave
Zora copied the story 100 times
Toni Morrison keeps trying to change the ending

In the end Alex Haley's Roots were sold
old artists look for their fortunes in fertile palms,
lose the ability to count their blessings
on Sunday

Seems like Lena sang Stormy Weather once
and the sky got stuck

Which reminds me: What is the present value of 1
billion dreams slit, sucked, scarred, riffed,
ripped?

B.B. King stopped lovin' having the blues years ago
keeps playing as a reminder

This is a never-ending story
an evolution
that will not
be televised

P.S. Back on the Block the brotha from another planet
watches Picasso sketch graffiti in the Subway.

CHAPTER THREE
WHY I SPEAK FROM THE WOUND IN MY MOUTH

Funk (for T.M.)

> I cling to the funk
> want to keep the kitchen in my hair,
> suck neckbones 'til they pop,
> talk shit with my girlfriends,
> eat Alaga syrup and granny's biscuits
> with my fingers, smell press 'n curl hair
> in a beauty shop on Saturday afternoon,
> stand around in my yard sayin' mothafucka this and mothafucka that
> laughin' at shit that's funny just because you jivin',
> dip in somebody's business
> and play the dozens for about an hour,
> find somebody who remembers the "signifyin' monkey,"
> go dancin' shakin' my booty and sweatin' until my feet hurt,
> and I smell like cheap wine, listen to
> B.B. King, Miles, the Funkadelic, and the Temptin' Temptations,
> singin' all the words off-key, forget
> about everything else 'cept how good it is to be
> black.
>
> (Weems, 1996, p. 21)

In her book *The Bluest Eye* (1972) Toni Morrison describes "funk" as something that Black folks who don't want to be Black try to get rid of—I cling to this Black-ness, this funk which counters the effluvium of institutionalized racism, homophobia, and sexism. I honor it, while acknowledging ambivalence toward the influence of white culture.

I want African American, Native American, Latino/a American, and Asian American students to get the kind of education that will facilitate imagination-intellectual development. I argue for the kind of thinking which is self-politically and morally critical—thinking which inspires students to take up dominant cultural forms of expression and put their own spin on them. It is critical to push students of color to create their own poetic-fictional-play-collage-type blues-rap, statements reflecting a lived cultural experience under oppression.

All students need this kind of imagination-intellectual growth. White students also need an intercultural K-12 public school experience with the following experiential goals: it honors diversity; it exposes them to all of the ethnic groups which make up America in a way that places an ongoing history of social injustice at the forefront of the conversation; and it invites the development of a social consciousness capable of envisioning a true participatory democracy.

With this book I add my voice to a long list of third generation Black feminist, and non-feminist poets, playwrights, novelists, and essayists. Political activists like Audre Lorde, Maya Angelou, Lucille Clifton, Pearl S. Cleague, Ntozake Shange, bell hooks, June Jordan, Alice Walker, Rita Dove, Toni Morrison, and Anna Deavere Smith. Women who create work that shows without telling, that challenges without offering solutions, that is part of an ongoing civil rights struggle.

I acknowledge a special connection to Deveare Smith. Deveare Smith's work searches for America's character by conducting interviews with people who've lived through a specific incident. For example, her work *Twilight: Los Angeles, 1992* about the L.A. riots and my work focuses on urban education reform. Yet we both put race at the center of the conversation. We explore issues of identity. We create performance texts which privilege lived experience, and cultural relevancy. We perform our plays making them accessible to a broad range of classes, cultures, and religions, increasing the possibilities for liberation.

I grew up in a family of artists. My mother worked in #2 pencil and watercolor, her subjects of choice the faces of famous, and not-so-famous people. Trips to the local Art Museum were free and we went as a family at least twice-a-year. Granny loved to doodle her own cartoon characters heads mostly, and my grandpa drew from real life, and played the guitar. As a young man he belonged to an all Black band that traveled the region. My grandparents and parents grew up during the pre-radio and radio era, and believed in reading, and conversation the two major forms of entertainment they were most familiar with. As a result, I developed a love for reading, discussion, and writing at an early age. This experience coupled with living in several poor neighborhoods all within a two-mile radius of my first home, where several community members either drew, or sang, or danced, or played instruments has more to do with my development as an artist-scholar than my public school experience. In fact, I've pursued advanced degrees largely in spite of public school rather than because of it.

I was not raised in an ideal family or community. We had plenty of problems: alcoholism, unemployment, my relationship with my mother was lousy during my adolescent years, and my father was not around to be a father to me, but my grandparents loved us, my granny always believed in me and told me my poetry was wonderful even though she admitted she didn't understand it. I received love and support from people in my neighborhood, community leaders, and many others along the way and they are responsible for helping me develop the self-love, and self-confidence to pursue my dreams. I've heard the Clarence Thomas myth that he pulled himself up by his bootstraps, that he did it all alone I don't believe it for one moment. My struggle has always been a collective one and I'd be nowhere without the people who've helped me along the way. I hope in some way this work honors their care and support.

"School Daze, School Daze, dear old golden rule days. reading and 'riting and 'rithmetic, talk to the tune of the history stick..."

K-12 School:
Granny made sure I could count to 10, print my name, read, and had memorized my address and telephone number before I started school.

Kindergarten: Old Dan has two eyes, Old Dan has one nose, Old Dan has one mouth, with many, many, many, many teeth. Miz' Washington, my Black kindergarten teacher in my all black neighborhood school loved us and I looked forward to going to school. After kindergarten, school was something I did because mama said I had to. I remember few of the details. Three stand out:

Junior High: 1968: Poetry contest. At 13, I was in love with Henry Wadsworth Longfellow's, Byron's, and Shakespeare's poetry, and was writing poetry to learn to love myself. That year I entered both the original and famous poet contest segments. I'd decided to perform Longfellow's "The Day is Done," and my poem "Death." Granny had altered her black, crepe dress so I could wear it and when I stepped out on the empty stage knowing that mama, granny, and my cousin Roz were sitting in the front row I remember thinking while the hem of my dress was shaking yes! I love this. I won 1ˢᵗ prize for my Longfellow recitation and 2ⁿᵈ prize for Death. That was the last year for poetry contests at my junior high school.

1968: Dr. Martin Luther King, Jr. was assassinated, and everybody got mad as hell.

12th Grade: Ms. Cosby taught the only hard class I took in school. She was a tall, slim African American teacher who was famous for failing seniors. Ms. Cosby introduced me to Shakespeare, and gave me my first difficult "A" on an English paper. I'd always made easy A's. I loved this class because Ms. Cosby challenged me to excel, she liked my poetry, and was always willing to talk about the things I was reading outside of class.

"This Revolution will not be televised." *(Gil Scott Heron)*

In high school, I developed a revolutionary, anti-white stance. I wore a fro, African garb, and wouldn't even wear white. I joined a high school level Black Nationalist group and quickly learned to be radical about being Black. I remember feeling angry as hell about the way my ancestors had been treated under slavery, and realizing that for the most part we were still slaves to a system that considered us only 3/5s human. Artist-scholars like the "Last Poets" and Gill Scott Heron were articulating these feelings through their poetry and music and arguing for political, social, and economic revolution. My disillusionment with several members of my Black radical group who were as much about exploiting their own people, as the racist, white folks' and system we were struggling against, and my entry into corporate America as a full-time employee where I learned that whites were real people too, and not all of them were racists constituted a critical turning point. I began to let go of my hatred for all whites, to construct what bell hooks calls a radical black subjectivity (1990, hooks, p. 20).

I interpret hooks' radical black subjectivity as articulating the kind of self-love that begins with recognizing your socio-cultural-economic position as a Black person in America; and continues with a conscious effort to develop a radical, resistive, activist identity which empowers. Like hooks, my work is an activist tool, a site of resistance. Hooks' description of an incident on an airplane which left her feeling a "killing rage" (1995, hooks, p.11) drags me back to my thirteen-year corporate experience with Chevrolet Motor Division as one of only *three* African Americans to work in their Cleveland, Ohio, Zone Sales Office between 1929 when it opened and its closing in 1986.

John the Bastard:
I started with Chevy at the age of 19 in 1974. The Urban League brotha gave me a reality check before I went for my first interview: "They're only hiring any blacks because Affirmative Action says they have to. Stay on your P's and Q's, be on time, don't share personal business and do your job, and you'll be okay."

I was radical in my dislike of white folks, defiant in my long skirts, red 'fro, and black boots and... scared shitless. A white man named John must have smelled this fear on me because he was always in my face making little touches on my arms, shoulders, my back, always making little quiet remarks about how cute and sexy I was, remarks which went unheard no matter which one of my white co-workers/ supervisors were around to hear them. It's like his sexual harassment was invisible and I was simply worthless. I regret 'til this day that I did absolutely nothing about it. I didn't protest, I didn't go to my supervisor, I just... took it until I was transferred out of Customer Service.

Art Doin' the Dog: (1980s)
Many Chevy office white folks tended to act a fool when they'd had too much to drink (not that they have that market cornered) so I always made it a point never to have too much at social functions. This particular year our office Christmas party was at a ritzy hotel and it was announced as a combination retirement party for a old, ugly mothafucka named Art who was retiring from his position (lowest on the management scale) as a retail, District Manager. Now, mind you this man had never said more than two words to me in the over 10 years we'd worked in the same office, but on this night did not seem to be able to keep out of my face. No one else seemed to notice, but every time I turned around there he was like a bleached English Bull Dog ready to be randy. Well I, no longer the scared young, Black woman, but still unwilling to be confrontational in an almost all-white setting, avoided, avoided, and avoided, until while I was standing in a circle of my co-workers, drink-in-hand doing the standing socializing thing I've always hated and felt something at my feet... I

looked down and there on all fours attempting to get his head at angle to look up my dress was Art. Without a sound I quickly stepped over his head moved through the room to pick up my coat and left. Nothing was ever said to me... Art came to the office several more times without looking in my direction.

The White Man (I've forgotten his *whole* name, a good sign?) who broke the camel's back (1986, my last year at Chevy):
New White boy in the office, big on the mucky-muck supervisor level said something I refused to hear with his eyes the first time he saw me. Not in my department, and not one of my immediate supervisors, it was pretty easy to avoid him, which I did as long as I could. One day in our new office which gave each of us little cubicles to work in, cubicles which kept our backs to whoever was approaching, I felt a hand lightly touch the back of my neck, then fast-move down my back in one motion. I turned just in time to see White man smile and turn to stroll toward his office. I closed my eyes seeing Louisiana-hot-sauce red, contemplating my fate since this dude had the power to fire me if I spoke up. Something in me said fuck it and I followed him to his office, closed his door and told him not to EVER touch me again, that I didn't like strangers touching me for any reason! Well, his face got bloody, I don't think he knew what hit him his expression one of total shock. I returned to my desk shaking, but so GODDAMN pleased with me, with the fact that finally I'd spoken up, I was ready for anything. Know what? Nothing ever happened, in fact, he transferred out not long after that and I heard his health deteriorated and his career moved downhill after Cleveland. My response: God don't like ugly.

RACISM IS SO PERSONAL

if it was a carcass
the stench would block
the nose of the world
and everybody would die

One billion pages printed
to support the myth

leak death over the fingertips
of scientific bullshit artists
working themselves into sweats
to meet the emancipation deadline

White power men wear their
Black face under judicial robes
making up new games with constantly
changing rules written in invisible ink
Injustice is so personal the woman
with the bandage over her eyes keeps
trying to take a nosedive

Way back in time today
the little white lie is a giant
wearing huge shit covered shoes
looking for a beanstalk
to fall down

Truth is so personal
every time it doesn't make sense
I sleep a little easier.

—Mary E. Weems

In 1986, Chevrolet Motor Division re-structured its entire Zone Sales Office division, and the Cleveland Office that had been open since 1929 closed. With thirteen years of service, several community college level courses under my belt but no degree, I was given the option of keeping my position rank and salary level and moving to Detroit to work in their Zone Sales Office. I'd been dying spiritually in that office for years, I was not using my creative abilities, I was not teaching, I was not publishing, I was just moving from day-to-day on a 8 a.m. to 5 p.m. treadmill—each day pretty much the same as the previous one—they all sucked. I was also in love—again, and thought I'd met the man I was going to spend the rest of my life with. Problem was he was a cross-country truck driver, unwilling to move, and he told me that he did not believe in long distance relationships, so I took the severance package and left. The next two years were hard.

With a business college certificate, and high school degree, I quickly found out that the 32K I'd been making at Chevrolet not to mention the benefit package would not be forthcoming. After several short-term positions, in 1988 I took a position with a small, African American law firm, where my boss's interest in my poetry, and his commitment to education changed my life. Over the next six months, he convinced me to return to college, and that I was not too old to pursue an advanced degree. With his mentoring, I decided to take a chance on me and returned to college part-time. When his office closed in 1992, I worked for 9 months as an Office Manager for a company that produced the Cleveland National Air Show, and when my position was eliminated I began attending Cleveland State University full time.

When I met Nuala Archer, a native Irish poet, and the only person I've ever met with a Ph.D. in poetry, our relationship changed my life.

1992: Damn, a real, live poet. Should I or shouldn't I? Something in the vibe between us said yes show her your poetry take a chance see what happens. I'd been writing poetry for 20 years and saving it under my bed in an old puzzle box granny'd given me. Only granny, my sisters and brother, and a few, close friends had ever read my work. When I asked Nuala if she'd be willing to read some of my stuff, she said she'd be glad to. I went into that box and pulled stuff I hadn't looked at in years. After all, poetry was something you did as a hobby, it wasn't something you earned a living doing. Ridiculous. The next class, Nuala asked if I'd stay after and speak with her... she kept me in her office for 2 hours! Told me I was a poet, that I had my own voice, and asked "Ok, so you've got it, now what are you going to do with it?" For me, that was it. I'd been heading for law school but thanks to Nuala's guidance and friendship I started submitting poetry for publication, and after she invited me to a poetry performance by five-time-Poetry Slam winner Patricia Smith, I started performing my work. As soon as I finished my undergraduate degree the following year I applied to and entered the Masters program in Creative Writing, and during my tenure as a graduate student, I began working with K-12 students in the Cleveland Public Schools as an activist artist educator interested in facilitating a love for reading and writing through the use of oral-literate, performance-

based workshops. Ultimately, Nuala and I became friends and though she later forever betrayed that friendship I will always be grateful because her influence, and mentoring pushed my life in a new, spiritually rewarding direction.

A year after I earned my M.A., I went to a conference and listened to an African American brotha speak to the problem of the low numbers of Black Ph.D.'s and his concern that as African Americans who earned Ph.D's in the 60s retired there wouldn't be enough of us to step up and secure the positions which would allow us to continue the struggle for justice. I decided to at least consider the idea. When I mentioned this to Ted Lardner, my thesis advisor at Cleveland State, he sent me to Carolyne White, who was a tenured professor in the education department, because he knew of the kinds of work she was doing as an urban education reformer in the Cleveland Public Schools. We clicked immediately, and once she had a chance to see my work and see me at work, she welcomed me into her circle of Jazz Freedom Fighters. One of Norm's former students, Carolyne too was appalled by the way students in inner city, urban environments were being mis-educated and we began to work together on a number of projects. Our personal and professional relationship, grounded in mutual respect and a love for this hard work, was strengthened when we realized during a conference in California that we were born on the same month and day. Today, I know that while we differ in skin color, and blood connection, she is my sister.

Carolyne knew I was committed to affecting positive changes in urban public schooling, and that I had absolutely no desire to leave Cleveland. One day (yes, this begins to sound like a fairy tale) out of nowhere, after I'd applied to and been accepted into the Ph.D. program at Cleveland State, Carolyne gets the idea that I should consider doing my doctoral work at the University of Illinois, her alma mater. My first reaction was no way in hell do I want to leave my home, my family lifeline, my artist community, my students, and everything I love! Well, Carolyne being Carolyne kept talking to me, and found a way to bring me to the University of Illinois to check it out. The poem that opens this section tells the rest. She brought me kicking and screaming to an incredibly supportive department headed by Jim Anderson.

"I teach the teachers I teach that you cannot bring Rembrandt into an inner city classroom where the students have only been exposed to graffiti."—Asian Student

When I raised my voice to critically challenge this institutionalized racist statement in a graduate-level seminar on aesthetics and the curriculum for future and current K-12 teachers, I was perceived as an angry, out-of-control, Black woman by my professor. She confronted me in the classroom, and ultimately sent me an e-mail stating that I could either respond in a way that was acceptable (no specific criteria for the mode of response was articulated) to her and some of the other students in the class, or physically remove myself and complete the course as an independent study. My immediate reaction was to be conciliatory, to ignore my "killing rage," to let the professor silence me—to get the grade, but one conversation with a friend made me see that I had to defend myself. I prepared addressed a memo to the professor's department telling my interpretation of what happened and my concerns. The department head agreed with me, but after speaking with their faculty member and determining that the professor and I had no common ground from which to begin a dialogue, the head recommended that I remove myself from the classroom and "write about it" which I did… it was a painful decision to make—I hated the idea that the white students who had e-mailed her to express their discomfort with me might believe they'd won when in fact all of us were losers.

This experience, which could be considered a negative aesthetic experience in the Deweyian sense, represents a break/gap in my work because I realized with the clarity of a bucket-of-ice-on-the-head that this kind of censorship and silencing was still possible in spite of the accomplishments of African Americans, and centuries of struggle against racism. Eurocentric notions of art are still privileged. Racism, institutionalized racism, cultural relevancy, language tolerance, caring, and compassion for students from diverse backgrounds must be a central focus in all teacher education programs. Traditional scholarship has been ineffective in promoting systemic change. It introduces important ideas, and theories; it challenges and critiques, *but* its audience is limited to other scholars. Performance texts that have the capacity to reach a broader audience on an emotive and critical level will continue to be the focus of my research and life's work.

FREEDOM

is an old joke they tell
at the Comedy Club on amateur
night and everybody laughs
until the lights go out
and they can't see the person
sitting next to them.

—Mary E. Weems

CHAPTER FOUR
DIRT: AN AUTOETHNOGRAPHIC PLAY

Character:
NUBY: An African American Woman in her 40s

Scene 1: Eminent Domain

(Nuby enters wearing an old brown, tweed cap. She sits down in the dirt sand box, tossing jacks down, beginning with her onesies, sing-song rhymes)
NUBY:
"Eeenie, Meenie, Minie, Mo, catch a niggah by the toe, if he holla let him go, eenie—meenie—minie—mo." *(Pause.)* "Ugly Black Nuby, sittin' on the fence, too damn black to have much sense." *(Pause while Nuby collects jacks in her hands and begins to address the audience.)* All my life I been teased about bein' what my look-alike uncle calls "black as the Ace of spades." Difference is—when my uncle says it he don't mean it the same way other people do when they just tryin' to be mean. My uncle told me that the Ace is the best card in the deck—and when I looked it up in the dictionary it said that it means you're the best at doin' somethin'. *(Pause.)* I LOVE my uncle. He's the one that stopped me from startin' to bow my head—from feelin' shamed. *(Pause.)* But the way I feel don't stop me from gettin' messed with—in school, at church—even at home where color's scattered through my family like jacks. *(As she describes each variation she tosses a jack on the floor behind her.)* My mother is light as milk and honey—my brother Tommy looks like somebody dumped in a little black coffee, and my sister Cindy has that "in between" look you see a lot on TV—sometimes it's hard to tell if the actor on the show, or the one pitchin' underwear, perfume, or fancy cars is black or what. *(Pause.)* Mama says I get my color from my daddy *(pause)* but I've never seen him, so I don't really know—she has a couple of pictures, she didn't tear up when he left her, but they're so blurred and scratched up—it's hard to see his face *(pause)* and my grandmother, mama's mother looks like white paper, except she has a flat nose and what mama calls "soup cooler" lips. *(Pause.)* I don't like it when mama says stuff like that—sometime I think she hates dark skin. *(Pause.)* Some time she makes me feel like she love Tommy and Cindy better than me. She always talkin' bout

they light eyes (even though they're the same color as mine), they GOOD hair—meanin' she don't have to rake the hot comb through it every Saturday mornin' like she does mine—and how pretty their skin is. *(Pause.)* When it come to me it's *(voice change to her mama's)* "Nuby get your black behind upstairs and use some of that Black & White cream on your face—I don't care what you say—it WILL make your skin lighter if I can ever get you to use it long enough!" *(Pause. Quietly:)* I don't care what she say, I showed that stuff to my uncle and he threw it in the garbage—told me my skin was always already pretty— that my skin say Africa—say freedom—say beautiful—and I don't have to do nothin' to it but live in it! *(Pause.)* At school, light skin kids get teased too—I hear 'em gettin' on my brother Tommy's case sometime callin' him white or "light, bright, damn near white" *(pause)* but somehow—it's different. When they tease me it feels like they don't like me because black is dirty—or I remind them of how black people been treated since slavery time—they call my head nappy because it's not more like white folks hair—when they crack on my nose and my lips and the palms of my hands—it's because I'm too AFRICAN lookin'. *(Pause.)* But I think they talk about my brother and some other light skin people I know because—they jealous! Mad because they wish they had fair skin and wrinkly hair, and odd color eyes, anything to make them less black and closer to white. *(Pause.)* Somethin' else I noticed too—they only keep teasin' the ones that won't be their friends, like my brother Tommy (he'll also whoop their butts, if they mess with him). It's like they want to belong to the "light, bright, damn near white club." Like it'll make them lighter, and somehow better than they already are. *(Pause.)* It's really crazy. *(Pause. Nuby gets up silently and picks up her jacks. Returns to center stage to face the audience.)* Last year I read that book by Frederick Douglass where he talks about what it was like to be a slave. *(Pause.)* My uncle told me that that's where all this teasin' and color difference started. He said the white man had to make somethin' special about all those babies he was makin'—plus, like Frederick Douglass said it was another way of makin' sure we'd never overcome. *(Pause.)* First, break up our families, then break us up by givin' light skinned slaves easier chores, or better clothes, or better food, or readin' and writin', or they own little track-a land— anything to make bein' dark seem bad—anything to make lovin' one another harder—anything to keep us back stabbin' each other—playin' jacks alone—talkin' to ourselves. *(Pause, and shift in mood.)* Grandpa used to talk to himself alot—but sometimes he'd talk to me. He used to say it was all about dirt—black folks in America that is—we didn't have any—and that's why white folks could treat us like they did. Grandpa had his own version of what happened, and he used to tell it to me on occasion sitting on the davenport in the living room right after taking a ice cold beer from what he called the ice box until the day he died. Oh yeah, and he always had on this cap. *(She touches the tip of the cap's brim. Her voice changes to grandpa's:)* Nuby, a long, long, long, time ago before any of us remember—we lived in Africa on land I can't even imagine how beautiful it must have been. We ran everything as far as the eye could see, and everything was dark, dark people, deep, dark dirt lush and sweet as new tobacco in a pack of Camels, and layered—you know like our people are—you strip down what we have on the surface of our dreams and we don't start having nightmares, or jumping out of windows NO—we just tap into all that strength, and chance for growth in our next layer, and when you pull that off we have another even blacker, even stronger layer under that— we are survivors and one thing America showed us when they dragged us over here is that we have more layers than we even knew—anyway some of our own people sold some of us into slavery, and a lot more of us were just snatched from the dirt at night and when we got here we were slaves for about 400 years, and finally we happened to get caught up in a big argument between the North and the South—unlike what they teach you in school though, Lincoln didn't free slaves because he was so concerned about our well being—it was a strategic move—me I think God came to him in the night and told him let these people go—Well, when they did, a white dude tried to do right by starting the 40 acres and a mule rule—but you can look around you and figure out about how far that went *(Pause. Nuby as grandpa kneels down in the dirt and picks up a handful letting it sift through his fingers.)* The bottom line is that even though today some of us own homes that sit on land, and businesses that sit on land, we don't really OWN one inch'a dirt in America—like the Native Americans they let us lease it, or sit on it like squatters—you think I'm lyin'? Well, let me tell you about something called eminent domain. *(Shift back to Nuby's voice as she takes off her cap.)* Grandpa would finish his story by telling me all about what he called the loophole that'll let white folks take back any square of dirt they want, all they have to do is come up with a "for the good of the community, or the many, or whatever they want to call it"

and bottom line is "poof!" what-you-thought-was-your dirt is snatched
and you're looking for a place to lay your head. For me it was a lot
more personal and up close—when I was growing up we didn't have
much of a playground to speak of—some dangerous pointy-headed,
swing-back-and-forth horses, one row of three swings, one of which
was always broke, and this supposed-to-be sand box filled with dirt.
(Pause.) Since I've gotten older, I come back to this box late at night—
when I feel disconnected from my spirit, or tired of forever trying to
re-invent myself, figure out who I am, and what I really want to do
with my life. *(Pause.)* I step into this dirt with my bare feet, dig my
toes in and pretend I'm back at home. *(Pause.)* We lost Grandpa in
1978... just before he died he gave me his favorite cap. *(Pause.)* Yesterday I finally took it to the hat shop for cleaning and when the hat man
reached inside to check the lining... *(she reaches inside)* he found a
little, hidden pocket with this pouch of dirt in it. *(It's on a string which
she hangs around her neck, then she picks up a handful of dirt carries it
into the next space)*

Scene 2: Love Hate Friendship Marriage

*(Nuby throws dirt into the space and enters. She picks up a broom from
the corner and sweeps it up into a piece of cardboard. She dumps it into
the flower pot, turns with the broom still in hand and begins)*
NUBY:
"Dearly beloved..."—SAY WHAT?—"We are gathered"
(Singing) "So We gather at the river, the beautiful, beautiful"
Let me tell you I never saw it rain so hard, rain comin' down in wed-
ding-balloon-fulls—one woman told me my life was set—the water
was lucky like the kind farmers pray for at drought time, you know
good luck, another woman—AN OLDER AND WISER ONE—told me
it meant gut-bucket luck.
"To Join"... In Americanese that means chained
"This Man"... AKA God's best friend, almost all powerful, wind maker
"And this woman" ME?
I was about as far from being a woman *(looks up)* Yep, Granny I hear
you say amen—as Africa is from Cleveland. I didn't a bit more know
what that meant for all the times I shouted the word at the top of my
lungs at Mama and anyone else who'd listen at every possible opportunity...

"In Holy Matrimony" *(stops, puts the broom back in the corner, picks up the flower pot and sits down.)* We weren't married—Michael and me I mean—any longer than a snowball in Hell. Even now I'm still trying to figure out what I did it for—I mean everything was cool—Maybe I'd seen one Barbie doll too many—Not in the I want-to-be-a very teeny waist, very white, non-genital specific, beach blanket bingo-blond, white woman, but the whole idea of having a man—which seemed to be the number one commodity through my teens and early 20s, Hell who am I fooling even my 30s—even now for a lot of us—marriage was like the captain on Star Trek used to say "OUR MIS-SION"—like a secret agent—I'd get up real early every two-week Saturday morning, drive across town to the only woman I thought could do my hair, and get my stuff fried, died and laid to the side for another two weeks, just so when Michael came to pick me up every hair'd be in place, just so at around 11 o'clock at night he could be doing his best to make my "DO" into a NEED-DO. I used to look at granny and grandpa all the time, sitting on the couch comfortable as two people who haven't really been two people for a long time, work hands lined, freckle-flecked, and joined like young lovers touching for the first time and say—this is what they mean in all of those magazines I see in the bins in the checkout lines, you know, the ones with the House Beautiful house dresses on, with that I've-been-married-since-I-completed-the-complimentary-4-years-of-college-and-I'm-JUST-so-happy look… Well, by the time the minister finished I knew I'd just made a terrible mistake, but I had no idea what to do, so I did what Granny used to call my duty—and tried to make everything else a lie, the wedding balloon water, that second woman, my stomach, the bottom of my feet, that long vacation my heart took, Hell I even told myself I was going to do wild stuff like, COOK, clean, WASH somebody else's draws'—I really didn't know WHO I was, approaching the American Dream sideways, trying to slip between the mirage and marriage like another word in the dictionary. I sat right on this stool the night I came home at 5 o'clock in the morning, smelling like I don't care, looking into a face that was worse than a stranger's. *(Pause.)* See I can't tell the usual—I can't pretend he was the bad guy, that he dogged me (well, only a little) or that I was little miss innocent because I wasn't—I was tired like a child who's been playing house all day and decides that it's time for her mama to come and clean up her mess so she can go take a bath, eat dinner and say night-night—It was almost as though as serious as I was when Michael proposed, when we spent all that money on a wedding my whole family didn't even want, when I half-stepped down that aisle in that white dress...that less than two years later I was somebody else. See what I didn't know then *(voice change to Michael)* Nuby you know you need to quit—tell these people what really happened... I never had a chance... YOU DIDN'T KNOW YOUR-SELF, Well you coulda fooled me—you ran me, our home, your life, you knew yourself way better than I did or maybe you're talking about some other imaginary-tall-fine-straight walking-fast talking Nuby? Plus, what do you mean you knew you made a mistake—we had a ball at our wedding, you danced until I thought you were going to rub your feet down, the ballerina slippers you had on so you wouldn't appear taller than me had skid marks on them... woman you defi-nitely have selective memory *(voice change to Nuby)* What are you do-ing here? I thought I told you when you moved out of here not to EVER step up in here again? AND You got your nerve—GET OUT of here... *(Pause. Nuby begins to slow shake the flower pot at a tilt so that the dirt comes out on the floor slow leaving a path as she walks slowly in a circle around the stool.)* I'm not intending to blame him though—we both left our trail of dirt—making it easy to find—little bits of dirt shaking into our clothes, our heads, our mouths until every time we talked all we did was cuss... I started changing clothes every few hours, using different voices, wearing wigs, filing my nails to points, disap-pearing for days at a time, coming home with no explanations, no conversations, AND telling myself all the time that I was just fine, fine as wine in fact *(voice change to Michael)* Yeah, you were so fine, the phone started ringing at 3 o'clock in the morning every night and the times I could get to the phone first all I heard was a loud moan." *(Pause.)* When we finally separated, when I had the divorce papers served on him at his job, he asked for and I gave him everything, everything that is but this one flower pot. *(Pause.)* When granny gave it to me on our wedding day it had a night blooming plant in it—she told me to keep fresh dirt in it with a few egg shells for fertilizer and to tell it I loved it everyday and the marriage would last as long as it should... *(She smiles.)* Wanna know something funny? For years I used to think she'd said it COULD, and I was thinking could meant until death—but a couple of days after Michael'd left I called granny to ask her if she wanted the pot back since I really didn't want a reminder of him, but I ALSO didn't want him to have it—I repeated what I thought she'd said and she just cracked up laughing told me: *(voice change to Granny)* "Listen, I know what you-can't-stop-this-from-happening-I-don't-care-what-you-do looks like and the very first time I saw you with that man I said Lord, this is it" but when I gave you that plant, I put a little something special in it, something you didn't know you needed—a little get out from under, get away magic—and what I said was "the marriage will last as long as it SHOULD" which in my opinion was for about 5 minutes. See you have to know and love yourself, you have to know who you are, what you want to do, how you're going to make it in this white mans' world before you can be married, AND you have to eat a little dirt before you can know all that—and at 28 you hadn't had anything but dust in your mouth." *(Nuby puts flower pot back on stool, picks up broom and begins sweeping dirt into the next room while she finishes the scene.)* Damn… she was so right—dust in my mouth, rusty knees, and so wet behind my ears I could have taken a bath. For me marriage was a short walk down a dirt road and I swore I'd never do it again *(she turns the broom upside down)* Until the next time…

Scene 3: Hopscotch

(Nuby steps into the hopscotch space and draws the hopscotch game with the broom handle in silence: she takes one hop begins while standing on one leg.)

NUBY:

My second marriage can be summed up in an epilogue: *(voice change to Granny)* Now I thought this one was alright—I even LIKED him. *(voice change to Michael)* I never understood why she left ME, I don't care what she said about why she divorced me! *(Pause. Voice change back to Nuby)* We were mismatched like a well-made and a raggedy shoe. I rolled around in his dirt for four years that lived like ten—I still wear his footsteps in my face—he left—I didn't laugh again for a year… *(jump to another square a little off balance.)* My first laugh was in a poem:

> The glass ceiling in corporate America was harder
> than my head
> I was on a roll rushing up to it real fast
> like a twirl dancer
> until they clipped my feet

and sent me packing trailing
blood in the dirt with my heels
in my brief case

(Quiet laugh.) Less than 30 days later I had the last laugh sweeping up my dirt, placing it in a safety deposit box so when I wanted to know where I'd been I could go in like a paying customer take a long whiff, dance back out into the fresh air and keep on stepping *(singing to the tune of "Nothing Can Stop Me")* "Nothing can stop me... so good do I feel inside got my bags I'm checking out because of you I only have my pride"... Stepped right through a bachelor's degree, my first book of poetry, my first play, my first look at the real me in the mirror, then like Will Smith says I got Jiggy with it... kept going to school and going and going and going a regular energizer bunny *(Pause.)* Months passed, years passed, I got past lots of tears—funny how some feelings move in and don't want to be evicted like bad tenants. *(Pause.)* Every time I thought I was over my second husband, I'd see blood on the street, or another one of my girlfriend's would tell me she and her husband had started falling apart and I'd feel myself going back through time kicking and screaming. *(Pause.)* Then one day (NOTHING) I mean nothing... I was in my car driving along thinking about my next gig, smiling about the last group of young kids I'd work with and it hit me like granny's hand across the back of my legs when I didn't clean the kitchen right. I realized I hadn't even thought of him not even a whisper in... I did not remember when. The next day I went to the bank and let them rent that safety deposit box to somebody else—after I flushed that dirt down the toilet that is.
(Nuby picks up the broom from the ground and begins erasing the hopscotch lines in the dirt, she begins a popular dance move into the next space then shifts to a slow following-the-funeral-casket-type walk.)

Scene 4: Dirt

Nuby:

(Singing:) Sometimes I feel like a motherless chile... sometimes I feel like a motherless chile... *(drifts off humming.)*
(Nuby looks up at the sky while standing by the grave. She walks over to a mound of dirt with a large cross standing on it, takes the bit of dirt from around her neck and adds it to the mound.)

It's not easy... being brown
brown the brown of snatched from dirt
nappy naps, little girl-game hand claps
vaselined legs after the switch
your switch the wiggly walk of all the women
before you comin' out slow floating down
to two feet already too close to ground
brown the brown of old bananas
old time rhythms, brown liquor drank
on front porches from North-to-South
brown the color of grown folks talkin' shut your mouth
brown bended knees at church, at hair pressin time,
at the funerals of all the brown women who've died
who've refused to die

Why do we look up when we want to talk to the people we love who've moved from the dirt to the air in a magic only God can know? *(Pause.)* Granny, it's funny—I learned so much about life, about being alive and treating people right—from you—you gave me everything you had you thought I'd need to make it in this world. Wish I coulda gave you more back—I felt like such a leech sometimes, always calling you with my problems, taking the first thing you said to me as my cue to spill my guts, never thinking that you may not want to hear my mess that day, or maybe you had you own on your mind *(Pause.)* 'Course you never said anything—just kept giving. *(Pause.)* You changed after grandpa died—I used to come and see you and feel like your spirit was running right before my eyes trying to find the road to grandpa, trying to get away. *(She sits on the mound facing the audience.)* When we put you in this dirt, I wanted to jump in too—so bad I could feel the dirt in my hair, smell the white flowers falling in my face, feel my nails break scratching to get in that last box with you, *(pause)* but after everybody left I felt a soft breeze blow across my whole body— I could smell your fresh-bread-smell, feel your arms in that air giving me a hug. I couldn't help but smile, this dirt opening like hands finished praying—your voice ringing in my ears telling me "Look Nuby, look inside find the dirt of your spirit, it's good, it's nurturing, gon' on sweetie pie—GROW! *(Nuby dances off stage)*

CHAPTER FIVE
GRAFFITI THIS! NO REMBRANDT IN THE HOOD (PLAY)

Characters:

SANDRA: (African American poet, 40s)

ONLY WHITE MILK: (5 glasses of whole white white milk played by one white female, 20s)

WOMAN PROFESSOR: (White woman, 40s)

SOON: (Asian student, 20s)

(Setting: New York City brick wall mural created by Jean Michel-Basquiat. Stage left classroom level square table with sign that says "classroom"— on top of the table 5 glasses of white milk: the table should be skirted so that the actor behind it is concealed until she pops up like a jack-in-the box to say her lines. Center stage a garbage can turned upside down. Sandra enters from stage left carrying a huge book which she places on the garbage can)

SANDRA:

(Singing:) "Mustang Sally (dunh dunh, dunh dunh dunh) I think I betta slow this mustang down" *(She stops in front of the mural, looks up at it and starts singing louder.)* "Mustang Sally! I think I betta slow this mustang down…" *(Stands in silence in a pregnant pause looking in awe at the mural, moving around to look at it from different angles.)* Wonder who in the hell named that shit horse? That's a laugh that ain't funny—calling something that works like Death's mama after something else that used to remind me of Kentucky Derbies, blue grass, rides in Central Park (the Central Park of 100 years ago that is) you know, the dreamy I'm-with-my-man kind. *(She's interrupted by sounds—a rapid fire of snippets from TV commercials, etc.—from behind the table.)*

ONLY WHITE MILK:

(Slaps his own face.) Thanks I needed that—You can face the world with confidence when you brush your teeth with Pepsodent, wash your face with Ivory, Ivory Soap, been so long since I had a tingle I forgot what it felt like, *(singing)* I'm dreaming of a white Christmas, Awww you can do anything but don't mess with my Blue suede shoes… *(Ducks down just as suddenly as Soon enters stage right unseen by Sandra, sets up an easel and exits, while Sandra continues as if she hadn't heard*

anything.)

SANDRA:

Or the one time my boyfriend took me horseback riding *(She picks up the garbage can as she speaks and takes it over to the side of the "classroom" table and sits facing the audience.)* I remember the feel of the horse's broad back under my behind, the look in her eyes (the horse rental guy said her name but her eyes said that wasn't it so I called her "Horsey") anyway riding Horsey as old as she was was like making love for the first time you don't quite know what to expect, but you LIKE the rhythm *(Soon returns and quietly places a Rembrandt self portrait on the easel and exits.)* Anyway, I don't know why I'm going there, this has absolutely nothing to do with why I'm here—*(OWM pops up again, but this time Sandra keeps right on talking so that you can't hear her, but she doesn't seem to notice.)*

ONLY WHITE MILK:

(Singing:) "Knights in white satin, never reaching the end," GOT MILK?, "I pledge allegiance to the flag of the United States of America and to the Republic for" *(Soon appears, both of them stand hands over their hearts as she chimes in)* "which it stands one Nation under God indivisible with liberty and justice for all." *(Soon and OWM disappear.)*

SANDRA:

So you, you see what I mean college really ain't about freedom, or justice, or the liberty to speak freely, to actually dialogue about what's real, about what's going on *(she starts singing what's going on)* "Motha, motha, there's too many of you crying, brotha, brotha, brotha there's far too many of you dying... you know we've got to find a way to bring some loving here today... " *(Pause.)* Love, compassion, mercy... maybe that was my first mistake—maybe I shoulda just stuck with the professor's script—you know, I thought I peeped her from day one, she was talking about sharing, and the arts, and new ways of approaching the curriculum—touching all the right words leaving me thinking that this would work, that I was in the right class even though AS USUAL I was the only... *(looks at the audience, realizes that they have no idea what she's talking about.)* Ya'll think I'm crazy don't you *(she laughs)* well guess what—I AM, but not in the way you think— maybe I should back up. *(backs up into the mural then turns around slowly to look at it.)* Isn't it something? *(With reverence.)* Jean Michel

Basquiat—damn, young brotha lived 28 years, creating, creating, creating, over and over—spelling out all the mothafuckas of his life, stabbing him in his head every day like his mission in life was to bleed from all extremities, like what was happening to him sucked so bad he had to paint himself out, paint black people out, paint how he saw us OUT on brick, canvass, cardboard, heroin tracks, leaving a forever body of work as difficult to read as a regular book for a blind person DAMN! Take this piece for example—he never named it—skeleton head in profile is what I see shot with uh—wait a minute—I wrote a poem about this piece it was the first one after all of the time I spent JUST Lookin at his work with my mouth hanging open—I could catch my breath long enough to write about. *(Takes the poem out of her pocket recites.)* This is called "Needles and Pins":

Chaotic-trap-capital-dis-H-hole and cube-shit-Afro-Carribean
swimming in a bone-fish-bowl
all his skin painted on walls-slats-stretch stuff,
teeth-dick-heads, H-deposits forming bone pockets every
place white gets in

He has one H-popeye that's not a black eye
no room at the inn
you have to put your nose in to see curiosity
killed, needle centers brain covers the crown
like a cap, all the rooms behind the eyes
get full of horses.

(Sandra pauses turns and stands with her back to the audience reaching up and running her hand over the image then turns back.) He was bad! and so good
(Soon enters stage right with an easel and speaks to the audience.)

Soon:

I teach the students I teach that you cannot bring Rembrandt into an inner city classroom where the students have only been exposed to graffiti. *(OWM pops up and they do a short chorus singing the line 3 times. Sandra is suddenly aware of both characters and begins by speaking to OWM.)*

SANDRA:

(She holds up her hand in "talk to the hand" position and says to OWM) What! Get back up here and let's talk about this. *(To Soon, loudly:)* What exactly do you mean by that? What's wrong with GRAFFITI? How do YOU know that ALL inner city kids have not been exposed to Rembrandt? *(She takes a step toward the Soon who looks surprised at the question and as if she has no idea what Sandra was talking about she doesn't answer because immediately Woman Professor steps out from stage right wearing a tee shirt which has "Woman Professor" printed on its front)*

WOMAN PROFESSOR:

I think I understand what she is trying to say.

SANDRA:

And what exactly is that? that inner city kids can't understand Rembrandt?

SANDRA, OWM, AND PROFESSOR (AS CHORUS):

(Director might use a recording of student voices here. The idea is to give the impression that they are all saying the same thing and that they are all agreeing with Soon, making Sandra the bad guy.) "I think I understand what she is trying to say."

SANDRA:

Well I don't. *(Pause).* I was one of those inner city students, I've worked with those inner city students and anything you take into suburban public schools, or private schools, you can take to them—you just might have to open your eyes, tune in to where they're coming from and be creative.

CHORUS:

"I think I understand what she is trying to say."

SANDRA:

Yeah, and that might be part of the problem, you all understand what she said without even considering trying it—maybe stepping out from behind the books and getting some FIELD experience would help.

CHORUS:

"I think I understand what she's trying to say."

(Sandra starts to continue but is stopped by the professor who is red faced and determined to exercise power and control over what she perceives as a dangerous situation.)

Woman Professor :

Sandra, I think you should let her finish—maybe you were too quick to react to what she said—

Sandra :

NO—actually everyone in here is responding to my question but her and I would like to hear what else she has to say.

Soon :

I was simply saying that I don't believe it is possible to introduce one of the great art masters to inner city kids when they have not had the opportunity to learn ways to interpret the work, they have no idea who the artist is or why his work is important. I ask you to remember that many of my students are from the suburbs and have no experience in the inner city. Many of them have had little contact with African American students. "I mean after all GRAFITTI is NOT recognized in society as great art." *(The last line is repeated 3 times in a religious-like chant by OWM/Woman Professor in a single voice. Soon joins in, while Sandra sits on the garbage can beside the classroom table listening—amazed.)*

Woman Professor :

So maybe we need to begin with graffiti and slowly work our way up to real art—is that what you're trying to say. *(Soon and Woman Professor nod their heads in unision.)*

Sandra :

Wait a minute! We've just spent the last two class periods discussing the fact that scholars have been trying and failing for centuries to answer the question: What is art? John Dewey said that art is created by the artist and experienced by the person viewing the art—as an artist I say none of us has the right to dictate to anyone—least of all K-12 students and their future teachers—what is or isn't art. Plus, have any of you ever heard of Jean Michel-Basquiat? *(Silence.)* One of the baddest, most innovative so-called "GRAFFITI" artists of the 20th century?

Soon :

No I have not.

Sandra :

Well check him out

Only White Milk :

Why should we? Anyone who knows real art whether they can DE-

FINE it or not knows that graffiti is merely primitive scrawlings—rough words and images which make absolutely no sense and break all of the rules of real art.

WOMAN PROFESSOR:

Well, it's about time for a break maybe we should come back to this subject at a later time. *(Stage darkens as Soon and OWM/Woman Professor walk off stage reciting:)* "...and to the Republic for which it stands one nation under God indivisible with liberty and justice for all."

SANDRA:

(To audience:) Okay so maybe I was loud, passionate is what I call it, maybe I shouldn't have asked Soon what she meant. After all, she's 25 raised in Japan (where they sell lots of stereotyped stuff about black people, you know mammie and pappy dolls), and probably doesn't even know why she thinks the way she does. This wasn't the first time I raised my voice in this class, and matter of fact, several white students had raised their voices a bunch of times—no problem—I was simply critically challenging her statement. I wanted to begin a discussion about cultural relevancy, the notion of high art being white folks' art—and people imitating what white folks think of as high art—and that everybody else's work is everything but—BUT my professor wasn't through—Me and Soon were cool in fact, had talked and been in small discussion groups more than once arguing, exchanging ideas, you know being part of a seminar for teachers and artist educators who want to incorporate aesthetic appreciation in to their curricula. But NOOOOOOO—the professor was upset and let me know it as soon as the break started—in fact before a single student had left the room.

(Woman Professor steps back out and walks real close to Sandra's face, they exchange words.)

WOMAN PROFESSOR:

Sandra, I think the way you behaved was inappropriate. You were angry—

SANDRA:

I was NOT angry.

WOMAN PROFESSOR:

Yes you were. You say you weren't but I could tell—

SANDRA:

I KNOW when I'm angry.

Woman Professor:

Listen, I'm just being honest with you—you backed Soon into a corner and I have a problem with that.

Sandra:

Well maybe I should just sit silently the rest of the class, I wasn't trying to disrespect your space—

Woman Professor:

Also you're too quick to shout racism—

Sandra:

NO I'm not, but Soon's statement WAS an example of institutionalized racism—

Woman Professor:

Soon is not a racist—

Sandra:

I'm not saying that she is and I didn't feel as though Soon felt I was backing her into a corner at all—

Woman Professor:

I think we should be getting back—maybe we can talk about this later—I'll talk to Soon—

Sandra:

NO I'll talk to Soon.

(Soon enters stage right and Sandra approaches her.)

Sandra:

Soon, I hope you didn't think I was angry with you—

Soon:

No I did not think that at all. I understand why you have to be the way you are. *(She reaches out to give Sandra a hug and they exit stage right together as OWM pops up from behind the classroom table and begins responding behind Sandra's back.)*

Only White Milk:

(With different voices, genders, etc., as Chorus:) Who does she think she is? I'm so sick of her, this is not a class about race, it's about art, I took my African American Studies requirements as an undergrad that was bad enough, why can't we just talk about real art?

(Stage darkens. After a pregnant pause Sandra re-enters saying in a straight voice rather than singing:)

Sandra:

"Mustang Sally, I think I better slow this mustang down, and down, and down..." Things got ugly after that. The next morning I received an e-mail from the professor informing me that my behavior was "inacceptable" to her and to some other students and that while she realized that Soon did not have a problem with me, she did. *(Pause.)* She said that unless I could respond in class in a way that was acceptable to her and to other members of the class, I could stop coming to class and she would be happy to accommodate me in other ways so that I would not have to compromise. She also acknowledged the integrity and unique perspective I brought to the class. *(Pause.)* I was shocked, hurt, and felt like the professor was concerned about her own feelings, Soon's feelings, and the white students' feelings but not my feelings—I responded to her e-mail at first offering to compromise—but something didn't sit right with me—it was the—the way she was trying to dictate HOW I responded in her class—and I don't mean that if I had been violent, or calling Soon a racist, or insulting the other students that she wouldn't have had every right to take this stance BUT because I RAISED my ONE voice to challenge another student's remark? I talked to my white friend, Linda, a music teacher with 27 years of teaching experience, the dissenting white voice in the class. She said she knew where I was coming from, but was not surprised at the reaction of the other white students. Next morning, I went to the head of her department and after speaking with her I took the Head's advice and removed myself because while she could see institutionalized racism at work she felt it would be counterproductive after speaking with the professor for me to remain. So I left—I went home and wrote poetry—see that's one way I struggle for change, it's how I begin to re-heal, it's how I share what it's like to try to make it at white universities—mostly I just felt… sad kinda like I was drowning. *(She backs up to the center of the wall and slides down to the floor spreading her legs wide and begins to pull a rainbow colored cloth from between her legs while reciting the poem "She Could Sing".:)*

That bird was singing
not when Maya wrote it
but just this morning
when I was feeling caged
spitting words that cussed
up and down the street
like I had a bull horn

I wanted to snatch that bird
feed it some of what I'd been fed
the day before the words
landing in my spirit
like huge river stones covered
with the green slime of years
and years of being lived on like
a side of rotten beef

I stopped and walked
up to the windows talking
to that bird like it had the answer
to my problem
I noticed details

the cage was neat and clean
covered with pink tissue paper
the swing was made of high polished
silver even the waste was deposited
in little cups that covered
the bottom

food and water were plentiful
hell she even had a tiny
stuffed person to play with

best of all she could sing
all day, all night
she could sing
she could sing
she could sing

(When Sandra says the last word of the poem, Soon walks out from stage right with her pointer and stands silently pointing at Sandra at the same time OWM rises slowly from behind the classroom table and stands looking. Black out.)

CHAPTER SIX
I.D. PAPERS

FATHER

His line on my birth certificate is blank

but he's in all the words
I don't say
my prayers each night.

I Am a Poem

The lines in my hands:
metaphor in a bucket
braid hair with words

wash my daughter's clothes in images

find one thing that is not
poetic, make it a poem
about a white man.

THERE I AM REDUCED TO A NOUN

Didn't Fanon have a mama, girl cousin, friend
girl, girlfriend, woman? Did he close his eyes,
hold his nose, hold his breath, hold
it?

Am I the 4-letter word
swimming in the white man's gaze?

Do I hold his head down?

Is nothing a Freudian slip?

Is it a secret code?

Is it a secret?

THE AFTER-LIFE OF FRANTZ FANON

The room is filled with black women
they stand the shades of trees covering
Fanon's stance like a huge brown sky

he rests in the dark
running his mind over his mind

the women watch the race
lift him with open palms

wake him up.

HOMEPLACE

The cool cut of a razor strop's tongue

a hugless house

mornings: lumpy grits

birthdays: blowout candles
lots of music, fruit punch, and I
get the first cut

thanks-giving: just a prayer away
and the light switch don't come on

Christmas: an aluminum foil tree
a plastic, 3-color wheel,
a plastic makeup kit

Welcome and Home Sweet Home
outside other peoples' doors

Never hearing "Yes" as an answer.

silence
is everything you want to say

I.D. Tags

A wedding ring is 1/2
of a set of ID tags

off-key moments
catch me staring in my
compact mirror
amazed at the colors

Love means never having to say:

Who am I?

I take several long trips
clap.

I am the double negative
trade my tag
for a pair of gold earrings.

Mix-up

Sistah mixes as she walks
wringer-washer hands
turn pieces of sky,
knots in her hair,
pajama pants, white
as Ivory soap.

Her fate flips
on the house flops
she's wearing
toilet paper soles
stick and lift
stick and lift
the ground.

She's around fifty
packaged in shelters,
political speeches,
church pulpits,
all missing the point

but she knows the punchline.

Her flak jacket
hangs from a shoulder
sweat is bullets
stuck in one pocket
ready for the gun.

THE WITCH IN SNOW WHITE

Today I hate mirrors.
Mirror, mirror on the wall who's the fairest of them all?

Niggas and flies I do despise, the more I see-a niggas the more
I like flies.

I found part of this story under Snow White's mattress after I gave
her the apple.

Snow White's daddy came to my parents' village
a long time ago (don't know exactly how old I am).
He was big and white and looked like something
They'd never saw before so they thought he was
one of the new gods. Oooooh they treated her daddy
and his people so good, fed em, gave em new
clothes to wear, gave them hugs. One night
Mr. White and his thugs waited until everybody was asleep
and snatched all the baby girls and boys (me included)
packed all of the gifts they'd been given, and left some
cheap beads and rocks piled up by the village fire.

Mr. White believed in writing everything down (you know
for history's sake) and when his ship was pulling away
from harbor at dawn, he tried to write out the sounds my people
made as they watched us slip away on some huge floating thing
white cloths catching the air and millions of hands at the same time.
Snow White's daddy died on the way back seems one of the
African boys from my village put a little something special
in his food to say thank you and when the ship got back
to Mr. White's homeland his wife gave me to Snow or as I like
to call her fairest-of-them-all-wanna-be as a
help-her pet.

Well, let me tell you when I read this I felt so hurt
I had to sit down and wait. All my places started

tightening up at once, my hair stopped growing, I stopped

breathing, my feet fell asleep, I just felt 6-feet under heavy
and then

I grinned.

No wonder! She never taught me to read and write, never gave
me a real name or let anybody call me anything but nigga
and ugly nigga when they got mad. No wonder she liked
to play the mirror game sitting one level higher than me who
had to sit on the floor at her feet holding one of her hand-me-down
mirrors to my face while she sat at her gilded vanity table holding
a gold mirror making me slap my face and recite my own insult
while she asked the same question and got the same answer
over and over.

Well now I could be glad about that apple, red as the blood I'd
spent in this place, red as her face when she took that first
bite red as rage! And while I'm packing, breaking mirrors,
and getting ready to get out of here you should know that
there won't be no Prince coming to wake her up
I put enough poison in that apple to kill
a horse!

P.S. The sistah who had never been a witch changed her name to
    Waking Beauty.

Making the African Black

the German, Italian, English, Polish, French, Jewish, Russian, Hungarian, Swedish, Yugoslavian... White

Return to sender
address unknown
no such number
no such zone

"If Elvis is King
Who's James Brown, God?"
                    —Amiri Baraka

Tupac and Dr. King jawjaking in mid-air:

Did you hear the one about making the African
Black, then calling this a colorblind society?

The light is blind
each morning it rises
to dress in the dark
leaves home wearing
mismatched socks
and the same clothes
no seeing eye dog or
red-tipped stick
spends all day bumping
into people.

A GIFT OF SHIT

Reverse discrimination, The Black Woman who stands statuesque on a Champaign corner making her home the air of the world as it races by holding its nose, the feel of campus on its way to praise the chief on game day, the World Church of the Creator its electric steeple shoved up the ass of America, looking at spit and remembering when it was against the law to meet the white man's gaze.

The Anatomy of Lynching

The civil rights movement
was televised.

Color TV followed.
After that a major, long-term, national
rope shortage called for racial rationalizing
and quick substitutes flooded the market:

driving while black drivebys, the tiny-rural-town
militia, good-ol-boy websites, extra long neckties,
the gangsta rap attack, recycling black-face
putting on a minstrel show that makes strange fruit
a pajama party.

Malcolm 10

What would he say?
eye bigger than sky
a puzzle shaking out confetti
reading graffiti
popcorn butter
video games

unfinished sentences

abstract-land

would Malcolm be surprised
to see his X on a cap
to hear a young brotha answer
the question with 10?

Language as Democracy

nominating words
orifices heading toward
polls make selections

they leave arm-in-arm
acting out change
forming paragraphs
on street corners.

DICK

I am not a crook!
I am not a crook
I am...

Damn! The man was lyin' so hard we, watching TV
thought his teeth were gon' fall out holding two fingers
up like popsickle sticks-licking his lips
showing us one last trick.

Much smarter than the Rabbit he gets out
before Easter
not wanting to be one
of the hunted.

AMBIGUITY

18 years of 85 words per minute
unorthodox finger positions
long nails to scratch
out

typing without thought
mistake

creating without thought
miracle.

More Than a Sign

Images appear and disappear
like moments, people we love, smoke
in a sun ray. It's hardly more than a sign
passes unnoticed millions of minutes, billions
of seconds

no second sight, no memory clip, no re-memory
signifying nothing in eyes going soft and fuzzy
crawling into technicolor spaces like it's safe
outside.

blood and sex is the daily fair
primetime translates Soaps
into something for washing

until blood becomes ink,
fucking is love
eye surgery's needed.

PHOTOGRAPHS TALK TOO

a tale of chiaroscuro slipping from the hand
that holds the camera's breath.
Pieces of film slick
as greased lightning
spill from the mouth of a politician

the eye moves like a pen and having writ
takes pause re-selecting, developing
themes hurrying to make an argument
that will be framed forever on someone's dresser,
or left like a lover at the bottom of the trash

one artist's trash is another's inspiration
the lost love of a pickup artist searching
in the junkyard of someone else's vision
seeing with a different eye

reproducing nothing.

Products Shake and Bake

bump and gang bang
rage on cloth napkins
spill guts in Spanglish,
Blanglish, Ripe mangos.

Round midnight all clatter
is reduced to the light at the end
of a cigarette, a naked bulb easing out,
streetlamps designed to come on at dusk
that don't

Every copy of Miss Manners is bloody

There is no balance
all checks are uncashed
all balls land like lead on heads
all sudden moves are acts

Living is underrated
and doesn't make the 11 o'clock news.

FACT:

A car hits a female
she dies at the scene.

Eyewitnesses recount:

Cab Driver:

A light blue '92 Beemer,
low rider with 8-spoke hubs, driven by a young white
guy wearing black shades ran over this real little
white girl wearing a red dress

Parent:

A dark blue car whizzed by me like it was going to a fire.
This old white man leaned out the window to holler at me
guess I wasn't moving fast enough and hit this young girl,
she was about 9 years-old, I think, cause she's about the same size
my daughter was at her age. I knew she was dead when I walked
up closer and saw that the white dress she had on was red,
soaking her up like a sponge.

The Driver:

Honest to God! I turned my head for a split second to answer my cell
phone... Next thing I knew...

I.D. Papers

1. As soon as I learned to write
   I learned to forge the letters of freedom.

   Paper was a problem.
   I'd steal one extra sheet
   each time.

   The next day one of us would disappear
   the dark a cover of love, a carriage,
   the papers moving through hands
   that couldn't read the signature.

   The last palm crosses itself,
   puts the papers in a safe place.

2. Today a white woman I've
   worked with for two years
   didn't see me
   when she asked me for help
   at the local K-Mart.

   Something in the air of all-white
   rooms makes me think:
   they want me to use the back door.

I still remember the drawl of the white woman
I overheard in a Country Club ladies lounge:
"ahm sweatin' like a ni'ger tryin' to read."

When I say Black is Beautiful, white men
tell me why this is not the right strategy.
At the university Thinking While Black,
is met with surprise.

3. I.D.?

My footprint-up-your-ass, skin
shed on application-this-and-fill-out-that,
the way I run my heels down, yo mama, the
blood I gave, how I'm found when I can't be seen,
the question before the wrong answer, social
security without any—when I say Mary, I give people
people the wrong impression.

The Day I Put Jesus Back

I still look up, but when I try to imagine God
as a man coming down to save us from all
our sins, I'm tossed in the ocean
unable to swim
unable to drown.

It started with a college class lecture
the professor talked about religion
like it was just another subject, took
me with him, the cross I'd never worn
shifted from neck to shoulders.

The next day it'd moved to my elbows,
slipped off my ring finger and
hit the floor as I dropped my in-class
exam on his desk.

Sunday a full church was closed when
I turned the doorknob. I went home and
read a book about strip poker. Opened the Bible
just before church let out, but couldn't read.

My fingers clumsily turned pages
looking for Psalms, verses, favorite God-folk

During the last lecture the professor
revealed he was agnostic. I raised my hand
to reveal that I didn't know what that was—when
he told me I thought him too?

CHAPTER SEVEN
SOUVENIRS

NOT HATRED

I understand:
not hatred
wearing a good guy hat
and a big smile

class divided like rooms
in a house, hate
a place to wear its hat:
funerals, cemeteries,
boardrooms

I understand standing
with both feet in an unmarked grave
rainbows bleached
celebrating special holidays
at the movies

I understand hurt:
stomach throat stop
moments heavy furniture

hope is the empty glass,
the make-do anthem,
a glass shard
sticking in the foot.

"The People of Illinois Welcome You"

comes right after the LYNCH ROAD sign
and the LYNCH ROAD sign comes right after

I see a thin road strung with the bodies
of black men like burned out lights
their backs twisting in the wind,
the road littered with try out ropes,
gleaned chicken parts, and cloth napkins
soiled wiping the lips of the audience.

I know roads don't hang,
but the welcome sandwiched between
the word like bread
cuts off my air
and I pull to the side of the road
loosen my collar

and search for bones.

Too Bad He Couldn't Fly

For: James Byrd, Jr.

body bent under the chain
from his back.
At the dash eyes spit
fill windshield with words,
watch for places
to hit over and over

agony was not one of the words

agony was the tailpipe of the car

agony was the tattered bird

drain-pipe-lopped, the hood ornament

for the car, the trophy for its driver

angry at being stopped
and given a speeding ticket.

I COLLECT KITCHEN TABLES

One table is dark, dark wood
thick-carved with pool ball-sized
corners, and feet for legs.
This was the table of a home-woman
she kept a copy of Emily Dickinson
under her mattress, read leaned-over
at night, kitchen table lit by old
electric light.

The Art Deco table is chrome
with a cherry-red, laminated top.
A 50s woman's, reads Hurston
stories, works one job
after another, takes night
classes in philosophy.

At granny's house her plain, gray
formica table always had a slight
dusting of powder like her face.
It smelled of biscuits, peach cobbler
crust, and licked icing bowls.
I can still see her hands wiping
over years of hand-made meals.

I keep her table at the foot of my bed
like an altar. It's where I kneel to pray.

Staples

an acupuncturist's needles
little pricks at the altar white as show.

the No! would not come so I held my smile
through all the colorless lies, snapshots
making forever out of the circus all the clowns
drinking champagne eating a cake that dripped like fear.

years later I hold this stapler in my hands
my fingerprints phrases written in shorthand,
I click the top like castanets hearing bells
that never rang.

TAMPON CLASS

The 10-cent tampon dispenser
in the state college john
is chipped, rusted, dented
white metal, slick
from fast fingerprints,
plucking the contents in a hurry.

The 25-cent tampon dispenser
in the downtown office building
is brass, engraved with insert
instructions. The product shoots
from the small side chute.

The 50-cent tampon dispenser
in the mall is black and chrome
with an invisible coin slot. It plays
music as coins drop and a secret door
opens, placing the tube in your hand

singing, thanks for bleeding.

INSPIRATION

sounds like a special
kind of sweat, that one-time
soaking-body-flash-flood

before you know it

you can ring out yourself
like a rag, your whole
head is a kitchen, and
absolutely nothing is cooking.

What's up doc? Stops
in your head and you
wonder what a rabbit is
doing on this river.

You float down yourself
noticing pieces of
shit, noticing that you're
changed to a single
drop of water.

Tangerines

bring her back, the juice
the sting of memory, her
blood, the way her hands held
together as she peeled.

Each layer careful as her love, each
section chewed and sucked through a face
I can't re-see.

At night I peel my own skin
the edges of my palms orange,
my fingers change to her fingers strange
at the ends of arms forming a circle
making a space to enter.

My eyes hurt from the smell
that's never her.

Baby Shoes

My legs open as an ocean, the blue light we were moved to changed my world forever. It was warm as she was, as new to me as she was, and both strange and familiar. Her first word was a sound that filled the space with a love so strong I didn't want her to go outside, or be touched, or even breathed on by anyone but her dad for 8 weeks. She was my split personality—nine months connected to my blood, bones like the river is connected to land. I carried her around for months too long as a toddler not wanting her to walk 'cause one day I knew she'd walk away. Today she's becoming her own song making mistakes I see because I've been there. She identifies part of me I identify part of her but we're no longer floating at opposite ends of the same cord. All I have left of that are a pair of baby shoes.

SOUVENIRS

"Bo pointin' to his nigga" is the caption

A lock of the black man's hair
sits inside a clean glass frame, on loan
from its place of honor—
the family mantel

There it sat at the center
of photos of birthdays, Christmases,
boys who went to 3 wars and didn't come
back men.

The image is familiar. My ancestors
swing at break neck speed

entertainment captured on postcards
a backdrop for hastily scribbled notes
of love and remembrance.

CHAPTER EIGHT
WINDOWS

WOMAN WITH YELLOW RECTANGLE MOUTH

You almost slapped my mouth off
but my face returned to the tree
my hands reach out blacker than
the last word blacker than right
blacker than the ace in the palm
of a winning hand my spirit returns
to land over and over shaping
the soil feeling the brown
in my back my mouth beating
like a heart my words burn
like a brand the land burning
hand burning the land burning
hand burning the land burning
my eye turns "of thee I sing"

Brotha with Blown Up Dreads
Wearing a Green Turtleneck

Mental dynamite is shit
holes in my natural
creative blobs
for mobs of
mind blowin think tanks
trying to figure out
what doesn't need
to be figured
there are holes in triggers
twisting my dread
twisting my dread
locks on images
spit from teeth that won't
begin again

there is no beginning and end
everything goes around
comes around
comes back

holes in my natural

"DO NOT CROSS" WHITE LINE

Even the desert flag
has lines of blood
spelling "do not cross"
on her floor like a
morse code

shadows cast her colors
like ship sails blow
from sky to ground
on Stevie Wonders' ribbon
they pull the stars down
to scatter

giving cacti something
to sigh for

the stripes are the old gold
of misplaced standards
the land wears a smiley face
funny color eyes

the Sun a single window
clings to light

BLACK WOMAN EGGHEAD

I am the original egghead
smooth obsidian cracked
smacked and bushwhacked
filled with knickknacks
that keep coming home
without a map
road signs
or keys

I play in the key of black
people turn me over
and over like a stone
make marks that disappear
in the sun

I cover the world in WE
while people build houses
of sticks and stones
bones bury and hollow
are numbered and identified
and each time it's me
each time it's me

I am the long playing album
the open space
the first eye to open
the last eye to shut
"every shut eye ain't sleep"
enemies rest on my face

I am everywhere
original.

Brotha Wearing Blood Hat w/City as Backdrop

Brothas
are missing in action
veterans unwelcomed home

wear years in their hair
like lint pickin it out
over and over waking up with
a new head full

every day the city steps
on their heads and they step
out step over step forward
learn to drill with one leg
run between buildings
look for friendly faces
find cop cars constantly changing
colors

but brothas
are always in season
brothas always need a reason

struggle "it's all in their heads"
covers their faces like rain
they keep their hands in
walk point
wear their wounds
under the latest
gear.

Brotha Smelling Something Foul

That foul smell
is a multi cultural
brick wall designed
to make A + B + C equal A.

it's like being the "artist
formerly known as"
breathing under a purple rain
another bullshot name change
rearranging the same pieces
remaking the same unfinished
puzzle

only funk
will clear the air

Skeleton Face Woman w/Purple Hair and Red Eye

Death gets complicated
like a rainbow
our flag is a bull's eye
and the seasons
make the hair color
like a coalition

we have many filled graves
Afro Sheen
all our teeth
a strong sense of smell
and all the time
in the word.

Brotha Wearing a Mask and a White Earring

If the Lone Ranger
had been a brotha
him and Tonto woulda
hooked up
kicked butt
and took the long way
Home.

NEEDLES AND PINS

"Mustang Sally, I think I betta slow this mustang down... "

Chaotic-trap-capital-dis-H-hole and cube-shit-Afro-Carribean
swimming in a bone-fish-bowl

all his skin painted on walls-slats-stretch stuff,
teeth-dick-heads, H-deposits forming bone pockets every
place white gets in

He has one H-popeye that's not a black eye
no room at the inn

you have to put your nose in to see curiosity
killed, needle centers brain covers the crown
like a cap, all the rooms behind the eyes
get full of horses

all the rooms behind the
eyes get full of
horses.

Memory Village

There is no ancestral place
in my lens, no creeping up
village fire, or special grasses, or trees
that whisper from thick spaces made for
a child to hide.

Everything stops and starts here and in 1600-something,
a time I have to be told about in old-old stories censored
for ears that can't really know shackles, swinging,
keeping eyes to the ground, making
sure you're inside at night.

My language is filled with holes that all start
with mama, and no-land, Africa a dream
too far away to smell.

I hear about people that still miss us
the lost children.

The clothes and toys, and pots, and spaces
we left behind wait quiet as a wish.
Africa washes off the shores and drifts
to us in lakes, and rivers, and ponds
that don't know how to translate
to a message we can understand.

Twist & Shout

All the streets are browner
than my one suit. These are thirdhand streets
bought and paid for in millions shot,
stale donuts and coffee, late nights
dressed better than the men.

Smells carry signatures and I can close
my eyes and say the names of each person
who passes before they say mine closely followed
by a question about my mama. These streets
twist on M&Ms that melt in mouths and
hands fulla too much time.

Here I walk in a way that tells my family tree,
turn my head to catch friends moving in and out
of storefronts that used to be upfront. Now
at after-ours-everybody-else's
this-and-that can be bought and sold
and nobody talks to police.

One shout bounces from corner-to-corner
like a pinball mixed in with the lies
of brothers.

At midnight the street rolls itself up like a
raggedy shade and

the password changes.

West Side Story

So much for whirling skirts, girly-shoes,
biker jackets, and boots, old gang
films about imaginary latinos and latinas
singing on streets that were never that clean.

During movie-making spectators wearing
everything-but-white and cloudy-day-shades
keep their surgeon's masks on breathing
in songs that roll out one after another
from the mouth of I-just-met-a-girl-named
Maria who's really Natalie, and white,
and knows nothing about this.

This is the stuff of pure bred pups
their pedigrees swimming in glasses of
this or that. Even the cameras
wallow slipping into dark spots between
cuts and action, the director spending his
days trying to get the film crew to get
serious.

Years later I don't remember the plot,
the acting, or the ending—but like to imagine
teens with nothing to do on a Friday night
catching this flick at the dollar show—throwing
crushed butts at the screen and leaving to do their making out
elsewhere.

MIRAGE

whispers caught in the air
with ghosts wearing circles
on their fingers like forget-me-nots
knots turning to vomit
first thing in the morning like a
a woman in her first tri-mester

the breakfast table is cordoned off
with bananas, separate newspapers,
individually wrapped sandwiches, and
briefcases marked his-if-not-hers

the two-car garage has a third car parked
outside where one of the parties
unable to utter goodnight and love you
in the same breath
escapes to the backseat
for a little peace and quiet
until morning

through everything I love you
is passed around on cards, big
red bows on birthdays, in short
spurts between church bells
on alternate Sundays at separate
but equal congregations, and

congratulations arrive every anniversary
from a host of friends and family
who never see them
as a couple.

LEFTOVERS

Eating is intimately connected to life
like air taking different shapes, and
smells it colors the breath, fills out the
body, makes everyone a member.

In one house left over eyes cover rice balls
with slime so slick it shifts and shapes
to shades of brown and green keeping
a stopper in front of the mouth. A mother's
hand knocks the block off and filth is
fillet mignon, maggot breath, the gravy
over breakfast, no lunch, and dinner.

In the new world she sets the table with
plastic says a prayer over used 1% milk
bottles, used tooth brushes, red spoons
and forks still carrying the lick of the
last meal. She gathers her family around the table
they bring their nightmares with them, create
daydreams eating nothing that can be killed,
borrowed, or stolen.

"Girls Are Maggots in the Rice"

When the last word fell from his lips
like chalk I could see his tongue
in 1,000 cuts, me standing watch
at the door of his family tree
denying Spring new leaves

I see years and years and years of no rice
in his eyes, nothing but maggots
fill the bowls of his cheeks
his palms slick with their spit
his feet slipping, their young bodies
break his sorry neck me
skinning his neck from the bone
I set it out to dry make a
wish on his back

trace each scar on the lives
of his sons.

Death Should Not Be Embarrassed

showing up for work
on time never late for his 5 o'clock
shadow

refusing to interrupt
a person in mid-sentence
before taking a breath

he doesn't dress funny either
and some days he's a woman
either way the color's grey
a pin striped suit with a grey
carnation, a charcoal sweater
dress, grey pearls at the neck,
a feather in the palm, no one
is tickled, no one turns red
when he knocks and when he
enters, everyone else rushes
out like they know the party
is over.

Circus

all over the world

people are dancing
to their graves doing moves
they'll never do again
dips turns flips
over Death's head mooning
showing their asses are stronger
than ashes

children in the act are especially
pissed off keep popping balloons
at odd moments, balloons filled
with last breaths scented with shit and
garlic

when their limbs tire
they pause mid-air to say another goodbye
triple-turn into each other's arms
and disappear in a puff
that's clearer than smoke.

CREMATION

It's not the fire. Death has already
happened the spirit gone to the last place
anyone would find it. To feel better we huddle
around her smell like love making sure
God doesn't change his mind. We remember
her dressed and dancing, her laugh
slipping off leaving calm
in every space she ever touched.
We are there for hours, the skin turning
to lash, then ash, the smoke clearing
a path for birds, dust, and slow whispers.
The weather wraps around what is always
left lifting and sending her spinning
away leaving
holes.

NOTES

Many of the poems in "I.D. Papers", "Souvenirs", and "Windows" exist because of my interaction with the following texts and visual art:

Albom, M. (1997). Mirage, Death should not be embarrassed, Circus. Inspired by: *Tuesdays with Morrie: An old man, a young man and life's greatest lesson.* 1st ed. New York: Doubleday.

Basquiat, Jean Michel. Needles and Pins inspired by his painting Untitled (Skull), in the Eli and Edyth L. Broad Collection, Los Angeles.

Benjamin, W. (1968). The work of art in the age of mechanical reproduction. *Illuminations.* New York: Schocken Press. (pp. 217—251)

Bonner, W. I'd like to acknowledge the influence of the work of African American artist Willie Bonner. The "Windows" series I created while looking at slides of his work represents a poetic epiphany, which took my work to another level.

Chrystos. (1995). Contemplating Racism. *Fugitive colors.* Cleveland, Ohio: Cleveland State University Press. (pp. 52—53)

Clifton, L. (1987). Why some people be mad at me sometime. *Next.* New York: BOA Editions, Ltd. (p. 20).

Denzin, N.K. (1997). *Interpretive ethnography.* London: Sage Publications, Inc.

Fanon, F. (1991). *Black skin, white masks.* (Translation). New York: Grove Weidenfeld.

Fuss, D. (1995). *Identification papers.* New York: Routledge.

Greene, M. (1995). *Releasing the imagination.* 1st ed. San Francisco: Jossey-Bass Publishers.

Hahn, K. (1995). Cuttings. *The unbearable heart.* New York: Kaya Production. (p. 30).

Hong Kingston, M. (1977). Leftovers, Girls are maggots in the rice, Cremation Inspired by: *A woman warrior: Memoirs of a girlhood among ghosts.* New York: Alfred A. Knopf.

Hong Kingston, M. (1989). Twist & Shout, West Side Story, Memory Village, Inspired by: *Tripmaster monkey: His fake life.* New York: Alfred A. Knopf

hooks, b. (1990). *Yearning: Race, gender, and cultural politics.* Boston: South End Press.

Lorde, A. (1978). Contact Lenses. *The black unicorn poems.* New York: W. W. Norton Company, Inc.

Read, A. (Ed.). (1996). *The fact of blackness: Frantz Fanon and visual representation.* Seattle: Bay Press.

Weigman, R. (1995). *American anatomies: Theorizing race and gender.* Durham: Duke University Press.

Zizek, S. (1992). Love thy Neighbor? No thanks! *Everything you always wanted to know about Lacan (but were afraid to ask Hitchcock).* London: Verso.

CHAPTER NINE
NURTURING THE IMAGINATION-INTELLECT

Students who enter urban public school kindergarten classrooms bring their races, religions, cultures, established dialects and/or first-languages, and viable, active imagination-intellects. They are well equipped to begin perceiving what Greene says are better ways of being in the world. Often, teachers who are afraid of difference do not welcome their diverse being-foundations and imagination-intellects. They do not view teaching as an art, and remain locked in pouring-in-knowledge-mode. These teachers establish straight row order silence, and focus on prescribed learning games, the alphabet, and songs. Before the empathy releasing the imagination makes possible per Greene, K-12 students need the opportunity to develop with educators dedicated to creating a caring, loving, reciprocal learning environment (see: Scheurich, 1998). A classroom environment which nurtures creative-critical thinking abilities.

As previously discussed in the "Utopia" chapter, I define the critical imagination-intellect as the seamless connection between the imagination and the intellect. For me, this process mirrors the operation of the heart pumping first blood through the main arteries, veins, and capillaries, and back to the heart—one cannot survive or operate without the other.

Unlike food, which when fed nurtures the body, fed knowledge sans a strong element of discovery, and cultural relevancy in a learning community environment, simply fills the student with contextual-less information. In this non-nurturing school space, personal creativity and several inextricable links are not made and Greene's "utopian thinking" is impossible. A shift is needed from constructing artificial separations between various aspects of education to recognizing and concentrating on connections as part of nurturing the imagination-intellects of K-12 students.

While, like Greene, I acknowledge the importance of exposure and interaction with all of the arts, my focus is the language arts and their connection to academic and life success. In her text *Fields of Play: Constructing an Academic Life*, Laurel Richardson (1997, p. 16) shared that the dichotomy between literature and science is a human construction that may be reconstructed, and that all writings use figurative language and narrative.

Here, I discuss the possibilities delineated in Maxine Greene's work for introducing students to the "not yet" of a more just, culturally inclusive, social world through aesthetic appreciation and expression using the lens of my own work. I consider nurturing the viable, critical imagination-intellects of urban public school students a foundation for academic success. Imagination-Intellection development is also crucial to the creation of the kinds of communities Greene perceives as the key to both national, social and urban education reform.

"I think, therefore I am"
—René Descartes

"I am who I am not yet"
—Maxine Greene

Descartes' quote resonates with the idea that the ability to think is *the* link to human existence. Greene reminds that being in the world is grounded always in the possibility of what has not yet been discovered of social and educative goals that are always just outside our reach, of the magic, wonder, and reason behind looking forward to another day of life.

Like Greene I believe that education through a culturally filtered aesthetic appreciation of the arts as the creations of human beings from diverse cultural backgrounds is key. As is aesthetic appreciation, that perceives the art of all cultures, as having a parallel value, and culturally filtered aesthetic expression, which I argue should be introduced and developed simultaneously, are the paths toward creative-critical thinking, being. And ultimately a more equitable society where all colors, cultures, and religions are embraced or at least acknowledged and respected.

While on the surface Greene's (1995, p. 113) work takes the traditional view that the imagination and the intellect are separate entities. And scholars utilize their intellects, but artists use their imaginations. Rather than what I perceive as the same imaginative-intellectual process with different end products, there are several places in her canon where she alludes to the inseparable link I envision. My theory disconnects from conventional beliefs about, and ambivalence toward, intellect as something separate from feeling and imagining.

My experiences as a student and as an activist artist educator in inner city public schools have convinced me that the majority of the students graduate mis-educated, without strong oral-literate abilities—without developed creative-critical thinking skills. This contributes as much as any other societal ill to maintaining injustice and the grossly inequitable balance of power in America.

Almost 30 years ago W.E.B. DuBois (1970, Foner, pp. 230–231) argued passionately and consistently for the fundamental right to a liberal arts education for all African Americans, an education he believed was key to our empowerment, to our ability to gauge the world based on our own perceptions after determining what so-called greater minds thought the world might be.

DuBois alluded to a "might be" which suggests the power to envision of Greene's "not yet." His insistence on a liberal arts focus implies a connection between the imagination and the intellect, and what he perceived as the primary imperative of the civil rights movement: to ensure that our children exit public schools with astute [imagination]-intellects able to conceptualize and work at achieving the "not yet."

Jonathan Kozol (1992) notes in his text of the same title that there is a "savage inequality" at work in America's urban public schools. Kozol's book focuses on the drastic distinctions in the distribution of resources between suburban and urban schools, and the resultant substandard education many students of color and a few poor whites receive. Yet, when the same term is applied to the lack of imagination-intellectual growth in these schools, this is another area where tremendous inequities exist.

My daughter recently pointed out that no creative writing courses are offered at her local high school, but they are available at the neighboring majority white high school. It is probable, as my experience suggests, that all public schools need some reform along the lines which Greene, other urban education reform proponents, and I am suggesting. But the level of mis-education in urban public schools where information feeding, not thinking, occurs is particularly alarming.

Professor James Anderson once asked in a history of education course: How do you measure the success or failure of the Holocaust? By the number of people who survived or the number of people who died? Apply this question to the practice of using the academic success of a few African American students to suggest that urban education reforms are not needed, that the playing field is level.

The powerless are denied the opportunity to learn the power and complexities of their own minds within the context of their culture, and how they connect and differ from the other peoples of the world. Is real change possible? Is it possible when, thanks to public schooling, you instead are trained to believe that, with the exception of a few, your place in the world was dictated and forever determined when America and its so-called democracy was founded?

If apathy and indifference which Greene (1995, p. 3) notes exists in abundance among the majority of the powerful members of the dominant group toward the oppressed remains, rather than the empathy we work toward, the not-so-wealthy will continue to act as though the education of "other peoples' children" (see: Delpit, 1995) is not their concern.

To echo Greene, once the five areas specific to imagination-intellectual development are introduced, once the imagination-intellect is released, the ways to expand it are limitless. All aspects of the media may be used as tools including: newspapers, film, websites, and music. The complex political and social underpinnings of media production and exposure are fertile ground for creative-critical thinking, discussion, and the creation of performance texts. For example, the preponderance of billboards advertising alcohol consumption in poor Black neighborhoods; the tobacco industries reverse psychology strategy of admonishing young people *not* to smoke; and the continued use of racial stereotypes in television commercials are all issues which stimulate socially conscious, imagination-intellectual growth.

The recent presidential election with its miscounted, uncounted, and un-cast votes could be used to explore the importance of having a one-person, one-vote voting system, and an educated voting citizenry committed to a true participatory democracy. In addition to research, open discussions, and debate, students could create performance texts that express their political stance on the subject.

The plight of gay-lesbian-bisexual-transgendered students is another area in which the imagination-intellect can be nurtured. All public school classrooms have many students who either remain safe in the closet, or are openly non-heterosexual and face ridicule, harassment, and violence. Avoiding this issue in public school results in high rates of suicide and high drop-out rates. It's important to find ways to use the published performance texts of a diverse group of young and adult gay-lesbian-bisexual and transgendered as a catalyst for discussion, and as a way of eliciting multiple interpretive responses. These political actions will go a long way toward creating a safe environment for these students, and toward reversing the stigma surrounding this lifestyle.

To facilitate student involvement in their public school experience, it is crucial to help them cast a critical, unflinching eye on urban education. This could be accomplished by introducing them to the latest ideas and research in the field making them aware of the history of common schools, their purpose, and the importance of producing enough low wage earners to support capitalism. Next students could be encouraged to create performance texts that challenge the current paradigm, which express their interpretation of their public school experience. The culturally responsive evaluations could then be performed for parents, school administration, the news media, and the community-at-large, prompting the kind of feeling-thinking that may shift the perception of the powerful from perceiving non-whites as "other peoples children" to our children.

The arts are a powerful way to counter apathy and encourage empathy. I nurture this emotional path to the Golden Rule in my own life through social consciousness, creative-critical thinking, creative writing, and performance. I encourage students of all ages through the sharing of prompted in-class and out-of-class creative writings based on life experiences and individual interpretations of a variety of artistic creations. For example, after viewing artist Sherman Alexie's film *Smoke Signals*, and reading his short fiction collection *The Lone Ranger and Tonto Fistfight in Heaven*, I wrote:

SMOKE SIGNALS

That day after the rage
watching water billow like clouds
screaming, the mist sending smoke signals,
the sound of my father's voice repeating
repeating "I didn't mean to, I didn't mean to,
I didn't mean to, his ashes mixing, reshaping,
remixing holding my hand like magic,
while I was lay down, feeling our sacred ground

the bridge over the water, our way back, way back
to before the white. After my father's ashes
changed the water to many shades of red, red,
red, red, all dead my ancestors washed my eyes,
joined my cries, after, after, after the rage!

I picked up our memories in the smoke signals
spilling from souls, my soul turning from stone
to flesh, turning from soul to flesh like poof,
like poof, like when my father said "poof" and all

the whites went away. After I screamed
our silence could not protect us, after
I painted my face in the colors of hope,
I started to hear the stories of Thomas
in the building of fires, in smoke
from the fires signaling my people to tell
our stories, to tell our stories in forever
fires one by one.

I went to my mother, with the word HOME
from my father's wallet, and re-became
her son her son her son...

—Mary E. Weems

Attempting to understand the Native American experience in America,
I began to realize the ways we are the same as human beings, as people
who want to be treated equitably.

I have facilitated these same kinds of connections in K-12 urban and
public school classrooms between students and students, students and
myself, and students and the teachers willing to take the risk of sharing,
of sharing power, of rejecting the position of knowledge-giver. Through
prompts like:

1. Remember the last time you lost someone you loved.
2. Tap into an early childhood memory, something you'll never forget.
3. Talk about something your mother, father, or other family member
   taught you as important.

students from diverse groups were able to discover that they shared some
of the same familial experiences and values. That where there were differences there was nothing to reject, but much to learn. Given the lack of
opportunities in a country which continues to be divided by race, sexual
orientation, class, bilingualism, and religion for interactions that cross these
boundaries, exploring empathy through the arts should be an integral
element in public school classrooms.

Apathy toward the othered, and the individual-based meritocracy
which is its co-partner, is grounded in the European worldview that traveled to America with the pilgrims.

Greene's work possesses an uncanny ability to not just talk-the-talk of
being willing to consider other ways of knowing. She has been able to

struggle with the tension between conflicting concepts, while realizing what grounds her own existential phenomenological philosophical position. As a descendant of African slaves I am drawn to a collective, communal-based way of knowing and being, a communality that's at the heart of why and how we survived. Lewis Gordon's book *Bad Faith and Antiblack Racism* (1995, p.5-6) argues that many Blacks are stuck in the what mode of being.

> "I yam what I yam and that's all that I yam."
> —Popeye

Belief is powerful, and I grew up in a poor, working class neighborhood believing that white folks were smart, rich, ruthless, blackfolks-hating aliens and as I grew older in the late 60s and early 70s I returned that hate with a vengeance. Granny called Black people "colored," Mama called Black people Negroes, I called Black people Black and later Afro-Americans, and one of Granpa's favorite sayings was "Niggas and flies I do despise the more I see'a niggas the more I like flies." What I was was nappy headed, worth less than a man, and different from whites—no one sat me down on their knee and told me this, and it wasn't a subject in school—Everything about my life said so. The only white people I saw up close were the police, and the insurance man who came by once a week to collect the 25 cents Granny paid for what turned out to be worthless life insurance. I don't recall ever being asked or asking myself who I was or who I was going to be, but I asked myself what I was going to do a lot and the "what" was always connected to a good job working for white folks.

In school who I was or could become was never addressed, but what I could become was everywhere. For years I was convinced that I was just like every other Black person in America, that like Popeye, I was already everything I was going to be, and hindsight being 20-20 I realize now that I worked real hard in some pretty self-destructive ways to prove to everybody I knew that I was never going to change. Change was a bad thing, it meant you got uppity, too big for your britches, it meant you forgot where you came from, it meant you were trying to be like white folks.

I hated school. Like the students being mis-educated in those same schools today, I had never heard that knowledge was power, that my ancestors both during and after slavery equated education with freedom and made tremendous sacrifices to try and secure real educations for their children. For me school was a place you went because you had to, homework was done because if you didn't bring home decent grades there was hell to pay. I stayed in the what mode right through Dr. King's "I am somebody," right through high school, right through decades of working for white folks.

Why is poverty erroneously linked to [imagination]-intellectual deficiency?

Greene's work in *Landscapes of Learning* (1978, p. 190) suggests that aesthetic appreciation is the starting place. Students first need to realize that human beings create art, before they are ready to explore their own creative expression. She defines "aesthetic literacy" as the ability to read different types of creative art including poetry, and other literary works, paintings, and dance. And to conceptualize them as only being fully realized when an aesthetically literate person interacts with them.

As a Deweyian, Greene believes that it is through aesthetic experiences with art that we investigate our lives and the lives of people from diverse cultures. It is how we move from the everyday experience of what is to Dewey's aesthetic experience the realization that each work of art is subject to a new interpretation by the individual who engages it.

Aesthetic appreciation and expression should be explored simultaneously in the classroom. The thinking that restricts what a student is exposed to or can learn in kindergarten should be re-thought. It is through aesthetic expression that appreciation becomes grounded in the child's life. For example, a group of students taken on a field trip to the museum see art lifted to the untouchable pedestal level. There is a sense of awe; there is a disconnecting from art as the creation of people, of art as something the student may be able to create. It parallels a kind of hero worship, where the worshiper is convinced that they could never do what their hero did. In the realm of public education this is counterproductive.

If, on the other hand, students are allowed to view a painting and paint, discuss, and write about what they see, if they are allowed to develop a dance that describes how they felt while viewing the picture, their imagination-intellects are stimulated. They experience the work of the artist, and their own creative process becomes the connection to their appreciation of their power to create.

The goals of the Black Arts Movement of the 1960s are pertinent here. Artist-scholars like Amiri Baraka, Nikki Giovanni, and Gil Scott Heron used their work to argue for critical race consciousness, and the power of a Black aesthetic in the struggle for civil and human rights. Artist-scholars and scholar-artists like bell hooks, Ntozake Shange, June Jordan, and Anna Deveare Smith continue this movement by using their work as political acts.

As an artist educator, one of the things I've heard over and over from K-12 students is that they hate to read and write. Public libraries in urban neighborhoods are filled with young people using computers to play video games—library books are rarely opened or read. The post-Pepsi generation prefers what they've been bombarded with at every turn, the visual language of violent computer games, television programs, commercials, music videos, and movies.

These students have been learn-to-readed to death, forced to read books that have little or no connection to their culture, or everyday lives, or areas of interest, forced to write based on a prescribed three-to-five paragraph formula. The purpose is vague and analytical, and expository writing is a chore rather than interesting or exciting.

What would happen if their introduction to speaking and writing were through their own power to make words say whatever they wanted them to say? If students realized the power of speaking and writing well and how reading provides the ingredients for becoming a more effective writer and performer?

Of course there are exceptions to every generalization. I do not suggest that I've never met or worked with a student who did not love to read and write. But the instances even in honors English classes have been far too few. One of the reasons students may dislike reading and writing is the lack of focus on the connection between orality and literacy. In public school classrooms the emphasis is on writing. Students are introduced to language on the page without learning that language is primarily oral, that writing is an imperfect attempt to reproduce speech and thought, and the original histories and stories of all cultures were passed down through an oral historian.

The dozens of oral-literate-performance based workshops I've facilitated in K-12 classrooms have convinced me that this connection needs to be made in kindergarten and reinforced throughout the student's public school career. If this link is made, students will learn what they are able to create by first reading a story, poem, or play, then finding ways to interact with the literature, increasing the chances to ignite a *love* of reading, writing, and performing. This is a passion I believe is key to imagination-intellectual development and academic success.

In one ninth-grade English class, I asked students to pick a poem and develop a skit around it by applying a real life situation, and including their own words. One group, a young man and two young women, took the Paul Lawrence Dunbar poem "Life for me ain't been no crystal stair" and created and performed a piece about a teenage couple who faced the dilemma of an unplanned pregnancy.

The young woman and man began the skit by practicing what they were going to say to convince the young woman's mother to let them keep the baby and get married. Next, the mother character entered, heard their argument, and recited the Hughes poem "Mother to Son" as her way of letting them know that their choice is a difficult one. These students experienced the oral-literate-performance connection through their imagination-intellects and the results were powerful.

The link between aesthetic appreciation and expression should include the fact that "(t)here are connections between film and literature, as there are between film and all other art" (1973, Greene, p. 194). For example, poets are inspired to create by paintings, dances, stories, photographs, and songs played on Greene's "blue guitars." Students in urban public school environments enter those schools with artistic ability and knowledge that should be welcomed into the classroom. Teachers should help them see that the so-called high art of museums, and concert halls, and so-called low or primitive art are artificial social constructs.

Rap *is* poetry. The flowin' that young, African American improvisational storytellers do in urban neighborhoods all over the country is a continuation of ancient, oral traditions. Their dances are connected to modern dance, ballet, folk dancing, and age-old tribal movement; their drawings, murals, cartoons, and graffiti are connected to the work that hangs in museums. How many of these students know, for example, that Picasso's most innovative work was inspired by a collection of African artifacts he stumbled upon by accident?

Free-writes, which I define as one of the warm-up exercises for the imagination-intellectual muscle, are another means of prompting oral-literate growth. I have used the same techniques with varying levels of success with K-12 students by first asking them to do short breathing and movement exercises to relax, and either giving them an oral prompt such as "remember the last time you were really surprised, what happened, what kind of day was it, who were you with." A sound prompt: whistling, chanting, a scream, a loud laugh, and asking them to write continuously for 10 minutes, and then share them with the class.

Improvisation facilitates, among other things, fast, creative-critical thinking key to the problem assessment, and solution abilities all artist-scholars possess. In one sixth-grade class, I asked the students to take a familiar fairy tale and update it to the 1990s. After the 15 minutes they were given to create a skit: one group of eight students shared "Snow White and the 7 Homeys" with the class. In this 1990s update, an African American, Snow White wasn't into doing housework and was letting the Homeys know this loud and clear. Once they reached an understanding, the cottage chores were divided among the Homeys, and the eight did a rap in a chorus line. The skit ended with Snow White sitting down to chill. The piece was humorous, creative, and the students took a classic fairy tale most would consider totally disconnected from their lives and made it their own.

Public schools continue to teach so-called Standard American English (SAE). I see SAE as a bastard, non-standard language, and to teach it without making connections between SAE and the dialects and languages many students enter public schools speaking continues to be a serious mistake. In her text *Talkin and Testifyin,* linguist Geneva Smitherman (1977, p. 2) defined African American English (AAE) as an Africanized English, a reflection of Black folks in America's linguistic-cultural Africanness, and the oppressive conditions in America. AAE is European-American speech with African nuances, tone, and meaning.

How many teachers in urban public schools are aware of Smitherman's work? How many believe, as linguists like Smitherman have always known, that all dialects and languages have a parallel value to SAE. How many use this fact to their advantage in their classrooms? How does the traditional view which still permeates public schools that non-SAE dialects are wrong, are bastardizations, affect a student of color's desire to develop strong oral-literate abilities?

To facilitate a love of reading, writing, and performing beginning where the students are linguistically may make learning to love to learn easier, and a lot more interesting. One way to accomplish this is to welcome the language-foundation students always already bring into the classroom. The students' languages and/or dialects are of parallel value to Standard American English (SAE), and this should be acknowledged in the classroom. Students should discover the connections between their dialect or language and SAE. One of the ways to do this is through aesthetic appreciation of the creative works of diverse cultures, and culturally specific oral and written aesthetic expression assignments.

How will teachers facilitate the nurturing of the imagination-intellect? How will they remain the strangers Greene (1973, p. 297) writes of, teachers who refuse to remain within conventional or traditional educative boundaries?

Reading Greene's "Teacher as Stranger" (1973) chapter in her text of the same title, I embraced Greene's argument for teachers who are willing to take risks that contribute to the intellectual freedom of their students. But for this to happen, teacher education courses must introduce the idea that teaching is an art. Future and current teachers need an awareness of the importance of seeking and implementing student ideas, of listening to student feedback, and evaluation. Teachers need exposure to the importance of improvisation to teaching strategies and lesson plans; of being willing to change direction mid-stream based on where the lesson does or does not take their learning community.

With this kind of background successful teachers will remain "strangers" during their teaching careers. They will develop techniques and ideas for nurturing the imagination-intellect in a collective, collaborative environment, making all members of their learning community partners in their educative experience.

Greene's "teacher as stranger" theory reminds me of the importance of having teachers in public schools who connect with their students, who the students do *not* view as strangers, but as people who care about them, their language, and their culture. We need teachers who are dedicated to helping students succeed "on their own [critical imagination-intellectual] journeys."

More teachers like the ones Gloria-Ladson Billings describes in *Dreamkeepers*, and James Scheurich discusses in his *HiPass* article, need to adopt what I call a spiritual approach based on love, mutual respect, and reciprocal learning. They need to be willing to step down from the traditional all-knowing-all-seeing-pedestal and admit to themselves and their students that when they teach they learn, that when students learn they teach. Students of all ages respond in a positive manner to being cared about, respected, and acknowledged as valuable members of their class.

These learning communities need safe physical and emotional spaces where the views and ideas of all are welcome. Teachers need to address issues of space, tolerance, and empathy for others with their students at the beginning of the school year. Teasing, put-downs, and the ridicule of their peers should not be tolerated and students should discover why through open discussion and self-discovery.

Students should be aided in discovering that learning does not begin and end in the classroom, but rather is an ongoing 24-7, lifelong process with opportunities available at home, in libraries, community centers, all forms of media, and social interaction.

For decades arts organizations like Young Audiences of Greater Cleveland, Inc. aware of the importance of the arts in the classroom have been instrumental in providing artists for short-term workshops and residencies. In these instances, either the teacher works with the artist, or the artist works alone while being observed by the teacher. While many would argue, and I agree that some exposure to the arts and its link to all learning is better than none—the problem is that there is no follow-up, and once the artist is gone the classroom returns back to normal.

As for the ideas I've shared throughout this chapter for nurturing the imagination-intellect, I think it is important to facilitate the implementation of ongoing relationships between artists, teachers, and students. I make the following low-cost or no-cost suggestions:

1. Teachers who do not possess what is traditionally considered the artistic talent of poets, dancers, painters, etc. should reach out to parents with artistic abilities asking them to come into the classroom and share, and work with the students.
2. They should learn which of their students are budding artists and allow these students to share with the class finding ways to integrate their abilities into daily lesson plans.
3. Once teachers are aware of a student's artistic ability they should find ways, for example, to get a student who loves to draw, but hates to write to make connections to the two creative forms. For example, a student could be allowed to draw out a creative writing prompt, to explain to the class what it was in the words that prompted his images. Then the teacher can help she or he discover that writers are inspired by visual art and why it's important to be able to do both.
4. Teachers with the help of school administrators should contact local community centers, churches, and art schools to locate and develop reciprocal learning relationships with local adult artists, and to encourage these artists to volunteer in their classrooms.

If you are a cartoon character like Popeye, it may be okay to remain frozen in "what," to believe that you begin as everything you will ever be. I envision a time when all students in urban public schools, from all socio-economic-cultural backgrounds, believe they are works in progress, and that they possess the oral-literate and performance abilities to contribute toward the better world they envision, abilities that help them move toward Greene's "I am who I am not yet," and radical, socially conscious, utopian thinking.

The book is an exemplar of and argues for using the arts and especially the language arts to facilitate imagination-intellectual development in public schools. The three performance texts are political acts that by existing, struggle against racism, sexism, classicism, and homophobia. They are self-politically and morally critical—they welcome co-performance, co-interpretation, and co-ownership. The texts invite jazz freedom fighters of all ages, cultures, and backgrounds to create performance texts that are political acts.

This work honors my ancestors. It honors all of the activists who have struggled and continue to work toward liberation. It speaks from a wound in my mouth as wide, as deep, and as red, as America.

Chapter Ten
Racism's So Personal: Invitations, Intersections, Interventions

Racism Is So Personal

if it was a carcass
the stench would block
the nose of the world
and everybody would die.

Mary's invitation is to write a personal, emotional response to this text. Writing from this white-skinned body, writing an embodied response to an embodied text, this response is as multi-layered and intersectional as is Mary's power-full, intervention-full text.

Mary Weems offers what I long for, she offers novel scholarly forms for inscribing and reading the social: forms that open different ways of knowing; forms that are accessible to wider audiences; forms that acknowledge writing as a moral decision that always involves the exercise of power, influence, and authority; forms that acknowledge the real physical, emotional, and moral consequences of scholarship in the lives of everyday people; forms that speak the truth to power with love; forms that honor particularity and universality while fostering solidarity; forms that facilitate the making of our own histories within the constraints of postmodern institutions; forms that breathe new life.

> When racialized ethnic diversity issues are discussed, it is usually within the confines of orthodox (conventional or radical Eurocentric perspectives)… rather than as attempts to develop ethnic diversity in logics of inquiry grounded in the indigenous experiences of people of color.[1]

Mary Weems offers bold scholarship written from a logic of inquiry informed by a literary jazz aesthetic[2] grounded in her indigenous experiences. Romare Bearden tells how his paintings were informed by a similar jazz aesthetic and logic of inquiry: "What I've attempted to do is establish a world through art in which the validity of my Negro experience could live and make its own logic."[3]

The master's tools will never dismantle the master's house.[4]

A jazz freedom fighter, Mary Weems' meaning is identical to her method. She models and argues for decolonizing research and pedagogical methodologies, methodologies that employ artistic creations to "energize world weary people,"[5] artistic creations that function as "raft[s] of hope, perception and entertainment that might help keep us afloat as we... negotiate the snags and whirlpools that mark America's vacillating course toward and away from the democratic ideal."[6] Like Ralph Ellison, she writes blues statements that improvise upon her materials "in the manner of a jazz musician putting a musical theme through a wild starburst of metamorphosis."[7]

From the vantage point of the colonized... the term 'research' is inextricably linked to European imperialism and colonialism... probably one of the dirtiest words in the indigenous world's vocabulary.[8]

Unabashedly, Mary Weems plays the dirty landscape of educational research. Digging into the dirt of racial memory, she invites the reader to explore a landscape of subjugated knowledge where everything is dark, dark people, deep, dark dirt lush and sweet as new tobacco in a pack of Camels, and layered. In this dirt we encounter the strength of African American survival and the illumination of another even blacker, even stronger layer as she invites us all to look inside and find the dirt of our spirits and grow collectively into new ways of knowing and being.

For the horrors of the American Negro's life there has been almost no language.[9]

Inventing a carefully situated poetically informed cultural praxis, energized by her mobilization of difference and multifaceted social critique, Mary Weems sifts and re-sifts the soil of her lived experience, and invites new knowing with each re-creation. Like Romare Bearden, her "combination of technique is in itself, eloquent of the sharp breaks, leaps in consciousness, distortions, paradoxes, reversals, telescoping of times and surreal blending of styles, values, hopes and dreams which characterize much of Negro American history. Through an act of creative will, [s]he blends strange... harmonies out of the shrill, indigenous dichotomies of American life and in doing so reflects the irrepressible thrust of a people to endure and keep its intimate sense of its own identity."[10]

The poetic act contains the necessities of revolutionary fervour which, for humanity, represent indispensable ingredients for the struggle for freedom.[11]

Mary's gift of deeply personal poetic communication inspires identification across multiple forms of socially constructed difference as it forges community. Like her jazz fore-sister, Billie Holiday's singing of "Strange Fruit" "compellingly stated the fact of lynching and passionately contested its cultural permanency," Mary Weems' poetic scholarship illuminates the intersections of race, class, and gender oppression as she bears witness to institutional racism and contests its cultural permanency; "where others fear to tread, she reaches out and touches, where others mask their eyes, she defiantly keeps hers open."[12] As she calls and recalls, plays and re-plays the same images, the stench is unmistakable. Feeling eclipses carefully constructed intellectual defense mechanisms as her reader is invited to feel, and feel, and feel through layers of cultural denial, into pain, into wide awake-ness, into the hope of warranted desperation.[13] This is art as defined by Toni Morrison, art that "represents the world that the artist inhabits" and enables... "some epiphany, some shock of recognition, some way in which one sees clearly... moves us a little further down a road that might be called real civilization."[14]

When the Raramuri Simarones of Mexico... offer thanks for the many gifts of life, they acknowledge the synchronistic partnerships responsible for their joy and fulfillment.[15]

A simple telephone call six years ago brings Mary Weems into my life. She invites me to a poetry performance and I invite Willie Bonner. Following a captivating and compelling poetic performance, we learn that Willie and Mary, indigenous Clevelanders from the same African American working class neighborhood, are graduates of the same high school; the first of multiple threads of invitation, intervention, and intersection that bind our three lives. Willie's painting referenced on page 78 symbolizes the magic of our synchronistic partnership (my face returned to the tree); symbolizes invitations, intersections, and interventions that merge into this book (my hands reach out blacker than the last word, my spirit returns to land over and over shaping the soil feeling the brown in my back); and symbolizes the terrorized landscape of America today (the land burning my eye turns 'of thee I sing'). A blend of oranges, reds, pinks, golds, purples, greens, browns, white, the painting is dominated by the black face of an

African American woman. Her head is topped with a gold turban, rich red lips are displaced to a tree, replaced with a golden rectangle, and a large black hand reaches out an invitation. Almost hidden in the background are scenes representing homeless people and a window with bars across a Bud Light label, signifies the mass marketing of alcoholism in inner city neighborhoods.

Inspired by the genius of jazz, listening to a blend of violins, guitar, classical instruments with the rap lyrics of Tupac Shakur, Willie creates this painting on the vibration of a logic of inquiry grounded in his indigenous experiences. At the moment Willie is creating the painting, Mary is in her first semester of doctoral study at the University of Illinois. Willie and I are in our first months of living in Flagstaff, Arizona, where I am in my first semester as the new chair of a teacher education department. As the university professor invites Mary to silence, the university bureaucracy invites me to silence, and the Flagstaff police invite Willie to silence. One evening as he walks home a policeman stops him and asks, "Where are you heading? We're looking for gangsters." Black skin + dreadlocks = gangster in this white man's imagination. Walking while black, thinking while black, and administering a university department as a white traitor… intersections… invitations for intervention.

Willie's painting fills a wall in my house and energizes my imagination. It reminds me daily of the wound of racism to all people, reminds me that silence is duplicity, reminds me to speak through the wound, to speak through the golden rectangle, to trust that speaking with love is heard.

> White people in this country will have quite enough to do in learning how to accept and love themselves… and when they have achieved this… the Negro problem will no longer exist, for it will no longer be needed.[16]

A gift of love. Willie's mantra is love, we must give love to all people, especially to those whose actions we experience as racist. This is the love Mary seeks to extend to Soon in her autoethnographic recreation of her experience in that university classroom. This is the love the professor cannot understand or foster because she is blinded by fear, a fear that reinterprets love as anger. Mary creates intervention-full scholarship from love, love of self, love of funk, love of community, love of social justice, love for the children, love that seeks to save this world by healing the wound of racism. She invites the same from her reader.

NOTES

1. John Stanfield, Ethnic Modeling in Qualitative Research. In N.K. Denzin & Y.S. Lincoln (eds.), *Handbook of Qualitative Research.* (Thousand Oaks, CA: Sage, 1994), p. 178.

2. Ralph Ellison, Toni Morrison, Ntozake Shange, Amiri Baraka, Albert Murray, Michael Harper, and Rita Dove are among the leaders of this literary jazz aesthetic. Romard Bearden, quoted in *Time Magazine, Special Issue: American Visions,* Spring 1997, p. 67, expressed this jazz aesthetic in his paintings: "Jazz has shown me the ways of achieving artistic structures that are personal."

3. Romare Bearden quoted in Lee Stephens Glazer, Signifying Identity: Art and Race in Romare Bearden's Projects. *Art Bulletin, 76* (no. 3, 1994), p. 414

4. Audre Lorde, The Master's Tools Will Never Dismantle the Master's House. In C. Moraga & G. Anzaldua (eds.), *This Bridge Called My Back: Writings by Radical Women of Color.* (New York: Kitchen Table: Women of Color Press, 1981), pp. 98–101.

5. Cornel West, *Race Matters.* (New York: Random House, 1993), p. 105.

6. Ralph Ellison, *The Invisible Man.* (New York: Vintage Books, 1947), p. xx–xxi.

7. *Ibid.,* p. xxiii.

8. Linda Tuhiwai Smith, *Decolonizing Methodologies: Research and Indigenous Peoples.* (New York: Zed Books Ltd., 1999), p. 1.

9. James Baldwin, *James Baldwin: Collected Essays.* (New York: The Library of America, 1998), p. 326.

10. Myron Schwatzman, *Romare Bearden: His Life and Art.* (New York: Harry N. Abrams, Inc., 1990), p. 30.

11. Paul Garon, *Blues and the Poetic Spirit.* (New York: Da Capa Press, Inc., 1975), p. 20.

12. Angela Y. Davis, *Blues Legacies and Black Feminism.* (New York: Pantheon, 1998), p. 194.

13. Guy Senese importantly distinguishes manic hope in the unjustifiable from warranted desperation: "There are many kinds of hope... one bad kind of hope is manic hope in the unjustifiable. While it is more immediately energizing than desperation, warranted desperation can *lead* to a form of hope realistically matched to the level of sacrifice needed to actually realize it. Warranted desperation is, in fact, righteously dangerous if it springs from an education about the abrogation of justice, fairness and opportunities for legitimate life chances" (p. 85). See Guy Senese, *Simulation Spectacle and the Ironies of Education Reform.* (Westport, Connecticut: Bergin & Garvey, 1995).

14. Toni Morrison quoted in CBS Sunday Morning News Television Show, July 13, 1997.

15. Don Jacobs, *Primal Awareness.* (Rochester, Vermont: Inner Traditions, 1998), p. ix.

16. James Baldwin, pp. 299–300.

EPILOGUE

The use of qualitative research expressed in experimental forms as political acts to promote social justice, and systemic urban education reform will continue. More African Americans, Native Americans, Latino/a Americans, Asian Americans, and responsible white traitors will enter the conversation. My imagination-intellectual construct will affect praxis among the activist teachers, professors, and administrators who embrace this idea.

I see performance texts created by the students who are being mis-educated in these schools. They will create work that is their culturally responsive evaluation of their public school experience, and/or other traumatic situations. I see more communication and collaboration between teachers and their students. I see more of these radical performance texts crossing race, class, and cultural lines. My next book will focus on the praxis of facilitating critical, imagination-intellectual development in public schools, and will be titled *Healing the Wound.* In it, I hope to integrate my performance texts, with student work, teacher work, and the writings of teacher education professors, and instructors.

The feeling-thinking elicited from engaging these interpretive works will prompt action. Ongoing dialogue among activists will lead to increased political action and systemic change. Our work will continue to be difficult within an institutionalized racist, sexist, homophobic foundation— our humanity will continue to exceed our ethnicity.

• • •

This Evolution Will Not Be Televised

One million poems, and blood
paintings pressed between fingers
not leaving prints

Picasso and the brotha from another planet
passing each other on a New York street,
the brotha pullin' his coat, Picasso
opening his trench to reveal his wares
hanging from the lining like cheap,
imitation watches

Meanwhile watching the fun ghosts
smoking huge dollar bills walk
down fast streets stepping on all
the cracks

Mothers create dance in large kitchens
with wooden floors, the mistress
of the house sits in the pantry quietly
taking notes

Contrary to popular belief Claude McKay's
tombstone does not say "fuck all you mothafuckas"
and James Brown was the Godfather of soul
before time started

Starting to look around can hurt if you black
and wonder why everybody carries
copies of your work in back pockets
while your paint brushes rest in jelly jars,
you canvas shop in the backs of grocery store
parking lots days food is delivered

Basquiat and Hendrix took a long trip
all their baggage was pawned the day
after they left

George Carlin said white folks should never,
ever play the blues their job is to give the blues
to blacks

Our image, our braids, our music, our mistakes,
our asses, our rhythms are played on TV
like a long 78 album in commercial after commercial

The Colonel in plantation-dress raps and moonwalks
selling a black woman's stolen fried chicken, black kids
snap their fingers, think that's so cool, bug their mamas
for extra-crispy

This is a never-ending story, that won't be televised
but:

Baraka already wrote a poem about it
Miles played it on the way to the grave
Zora copied the story 100 times
Toni Morrison keeps trying to change the ending

In the end Alex Haley's Roots were sold
old artists look for their fortunes in fertile palms,
lose the ability to count their blessings
on Sunday

Seems like Lena sang Stormy Weather once
and the sky got stuck

Which reminds me: What is the present value of 1
billion dreams slit, sucked, scarred, riffed,
ripped?

B.B. King stopped lovin' having the blues years ago
keeps playing as a reminder

This is a never-ending story
an evolution
that will not
be televised

P.S. Back on the Block the brotha from another planet
watches Picasso sketch graffiti in the Subway.

—Mary E. Weems

BIBLIOGRAPHY

Abu-Jamal, M. (1997). *Death blossoms*. Farmington: The Plough Publishing House of the Bruderhof Foundation.

Alexie, S. (1993). *The Lone Ranger and Tonto fistfight in heaven*. New York: HarperCollins Publishers, Inc.

Algarin, M., & Holman, B. (Eds.) (1994). *Aloud: Voices from the nuyorican poets café*. New York, NY: Henry Holt and Company.

Alston, K. (1993a). Community politics and the education of African American males: Whose life is it anyway? In Catherine Marshall (ed). *New politics of race and gender*. pp. 117–127. London: Falmer Press.

Alston, K. (1993b). The pragmatics and politics of difference. *Midwest Modern Language Association Journal* pp. 587–74.

Alston, K. (1995). Begging the question: Is critical thinking biased? *Educational Theory*, 45, (2), pp. 225–233.

Alston, K. (1998a). Give me love, crazy love: Or why teachers are not like analysts. *Philosophy of Education*, pp. 366–369.

Alston, K. (1998b). Hands off consensual sex. *Academe*. v. 84, no. 5, pp. 32–33.

Ayers, W.C., & Miller, J. L. (Eds.) (1998). *A light in dark times: Maxine Greene and the unfinished conversation*. New York, NY: Teachers College Press.

Baraka, A. (1995). *Transbluesency*. New York: Marsilio Publishers, Corp.

Beach, R., & Finders, M. J. (1999). Students as ethnographers: Guiding alternative research projects. *English Journal, 89*, (1), pp. 82–90.

Bourdieu, P. (1993). *The field of cultural production*. New York: Columbia University Press.

Brown, A. L. (1998). *Subjects of deceit: A phenomenology of lying*. Albany: State University of New York.

Brown, C. S. (1992). *Ready from within: Septima Clark and the civil rights movement*. Trenton: Africa World Press.

Clifford, J. (1997). *Routes*. Cambridge: Harvard University Press.

Delpit, L. (1995). *Other people's children: Cultural conflict in the classroom*. New York: The New Press.

Denzin, N.K. (1984). *On understanding emotion*. (1st ed.) Jossey-Bass Social and Behavioral Science Series. San Francisco: Jossey-Bass, Inc.

Denzin, N. K. (1991a). *Images of postmodern society: Social theory and contemporary cinema*. London: Sage Publications, Inc.

Denzin, N. K. (1991b). The postmodern sexual order: Sex, lies, and yuppie (Examination of *Sex, Lies, and Videotape* and *When Harry Met Sally*). *Social Science Journal, 28*, (3), pp. 407–424.

Denzin, N. K. (1995). *The cinematic society: The voyeur's gaze*. London: Sage Publications, Inc.

Denzin, N. K. (1997a). Reading Scheff's vision of sociology. *Sociological Perspectives*, 40, (4), pp. 548–550.

Denzin, N. K. (1997b). *Interpretive ethnography: Ethnographic practices for the 21st century*. London: Sage Publications, Inc.

Denzin, N. K. (1999). Interpretive ethnography for the next century. *Journal of Contemporary Ethnography, 28*, (5), pp. 510–519.

Denzin, N. K., & Lincoln, Y. S. (Eds.). (1994). *Handbook of qualitative research*. (2nd Ed.). London: Sage Publications, Inc.

Denzin, N. K. , & Lincoln, Y. S. (Eds.). (2000). The seventh moment. *Handbook of qualitative research*. London: Sage Publications, Inc.

Deveare, A.D. *Twilight: Los Angeles, 1992*. New York: Anchor Books, Doubleday.

Dewey, J. (1900). *The child and the curriculum*. Chicago: University of Chicago Press.

Dewey, J. (Ed.) (1916). *Democracy and education*. New York: Free Press.

Dewey, J. (1934). *Art as experience*. New York: Capricorn Books.

Dillard, A. (1982). *Teaching a stone to talk: Expeditions and encounters*. New York: HarperCollins Publishers, Inc.

Foner, Philip S. (Ed.). (1970). *W.E.B. DuBois speaks: Speeches and addresses*. New York: Pathfinder Press.

Freire, P. (1985). *The politics of education*. South Hadley, MA: Bergin & Garvey Publishers, Inc.

Friedman, E. G., & Squire, C. (Eds.). (1998). "lite." *Morality usa*. Minneapolis: University of Minnesota Press. (pp. 190–215).

Gilroy, P. (1993). The Black Atlantic as a counterculture of modernity. In P. Gilroy, *The Black Atlantic: Modernity and double consciousness*. Cambridge: Harvard University Press. (pp. 1–40).

Gilyard, K. (Ed.). (1997). *Spirit & flame: An anthology of contemporary African American poetry*. Syracuse: Syracuse University Press.

Giroux, H. (1983). *Theory and resistance in education: A pedagogy for the opposition*. South Hadley, MA: Bergin & Garvey.

Giroux, H. (1988). Critical theory and the politics of culture and voice: Rethinking the discourse of educational research. In R. Sherman & R. Webb (Eds.), *Qualitative research in education: Focus and methods* (pp. 190–210). New York: Falmer.

Giroux, H. (1992). *Border crossings: Cultural workers and the politics of education*. New York: Routledge.

Giroux, H. (1997). *Pedagogy and the politics of hope: Theory, culture, and schooling*. Boulder, CO: Westview.

Gordon, L. (1995). *Bad faith and anti-black racism*. Atlantic Highlands, NJ: Humanities Press International, Inc.

Greene, M. (1965). *Public schools and the private vision*. New York, NY: Random House, Inc.

Greene, M. (1973). *Teacher as stranger: Educational philosophy for the modern age*. Belmont,

CA: Wadsworth Publishing Company.

Greene, M. (1978). *Landscapes of learning*. New York: NY: Teachers College Press.

Greene, M. (1988). *The dialectic of freedom*. New York, NY: Teachers College Press.

Greene, M. (1995). *Releasing the imagination*. San Francisco, CA: Jossey-Bass, Inc.

Groening, M. (1987). *School is hell*. (p. 1). New York: Pantheon Books.

Hall, S. (1994). Cultural studies: Two paradigms. In N. Dirks et al. (Eds.) *Culture/power/ history: A reader in contemporary social theory*. Princeton: Princeton University Press. pp. 521–538

Hofstader, R. (1962). *Anti-intellectualism in American life*. New York: Vintage Books, a Division of Random House.

Hong Kingston, M. (1975). *A woman warrior: Memoirs of a girlhood among ghosts*. New York: Alfred A. Knopf, Inc.

hooks, b. (1981). *Ain't I a woman: Black women and feminism*. Boston, MA: South End Press.

hooks, b. (1984). *Feminist theory from margin to center*. Boston, MA: South End Press.

hooks, b. (1990). *Yearning: Race, gender, and cultural politics*. Boston, MA: South End Press.

hooks, b. (1994). *Teaching to transgress*. New York: Routledge.

hooks, b. (1995). *Killing rage: Ending racism*. (1st Ed.). New York: H. Holt and Company.

Howard, J., & Hammond., R. (1985). Rumors of inferiority: The hidden obstacles to black success. *The New Republic*, pp. 17–21.

Jefferson, T. (1776). The Declaration of Independence. *The Indiana University School of Law*. Retrieved December 5, 2000 from the World Wide Web: *http:// www.law.indiana.edu/uslawdocs/declaration.html*

Jordan, J. (1994). *Affirmative acts*. New York: Bantam Doubleday Dell Publishing Group, Inc.

Kincheloe, J.L. (1991). *Teachers as researchers: Qualitative paths to empowerment*. London: Falmer.

Kincheloe, J.L. (1993). *Toward a critical politics of teacher thinking: Mapping the postmodern*. Granby, MA: Bergin & Garvey.

Kozol, J. (1992). *Savage inequality: Children in America's schools*. New York: HarperCollins Publishers, Inc.

Ladson-Billings, G. (1994). *Dreamkeepers*. San Francisco: Jossey Bass, Inc., Publishers.

Larabee, D. F. (1997). Public goods, private goods: The American struggle over educational goals. *American Educational Research Journal, 34*, (1), pp. 39–81.

Lorde, A. (1978). *The black unicorn*. New York: W. W. Norton & Company, Inc.

Lorde, A. (1984). *Sister outsider*. Freedom, CA: The Crossing Press.

Lorde, A. (1985) *I am your sister: Black women organizing across sexualities*. (1st Ed.). New York: Kitchen Table, Women of Color Press.

Lorde, A. (1988). *A burst of light: Essays*. Ithaca, NY: Firebrand Books.

Lorde, A. (1992). *Undersong: Chosen poems old and new revised.* New York: W.W. Norton & Company.

Lorde, A. (1993). *Poetry is not a luxury.* Osnabruck, Germany: Druck & Verlags Cooperative.

McClaren, P. (1995a). *Critical pedagogy and predatory culture: Oppositional politics in a postmodern era.* New York: Routledge.

McLaren, P. (1995b). *Life in schools* (3rd ed.). New York: Longman.

McLaren, P. (1997). *Revolutionary multiculturalism: Pedagogies of dissent for the new millennium.* New York: Routledge.

McLaren, P. (1998). Revolutionary pedagogy in post-revolutionary times: Rethinking the political economy of critical education. *Education Theory, 48,* 431–462.

Morrison, T. (1972). *The bluest eye.* New York: Pocket Books.

Murray, A. (1996). *The blue devils of nada: A contemporary American approach to aesthetic statement.* New York: Pantheon Books.

Noblitt, G. (1999). The possibilities of postcritical ethnographies: An introduction to this issue. *Educational Foundations, 13,* (1), pp. 3–6.

On, B.A. Bar, & Ferguson, A. (Eds.). (1998). *Daring to be good: Essays in feminist ethico-politics.* Heldke, Lisa. "On being a responsible traitor: A primer." New York: Routledge.

Pinar, W. F. (Ed.). (1998). *The passionate mind of Maxine Greene: 'I am not yet.'* Bristol, PA: Falmer Press, Taylor & Francis, Inc.

Richardson, L. (1997). *Fields of play: Constructing an academic life.* New Brunswick, NJ: Rutgers University Press.

Roberts, C. (1993) Cultural studies and student exchange: Living the ethnographic life. *Language Culture & Curriculum, 6,* (1), pp. 11–17.

Scheurich, J. J. (1998). Highly successful and loving, public elementary schools populated mainly By low-SES children of color: Core beliefs and cultural characteristics. *Urban Education,* vol. 33, No. 4, November, 1998.

Smith, A. D. (1994). *Twilight: Los Angeles, 1992.* New York: Anchor Books, Doubleday.

Smitherman, G. (1977). *Talkin and testifyin.* Detroit Michigan: Wayne State University Press.

Vangelisti, P. (1995). *The selected poems of Amira Baraka/Leroi Jones (1961–1995).* New York, New York: Marsilio Publishers.

Weems, M. E. Funk. (1996). *White.* Wick Chapbook Series Two, no. 2. Kent, Ohio: Kent State University Press.

Weems, M. (1998). "Utopia, imagination-intellect as a pedagogical focus." (unpublished paper).

White, C. J. (1995). Does "Proper social theory" require a reconstructive intent? In R. Brossio (ed.), *Philosophical studies in education: Proceedings of annual meeting of the Ohio valley Philosophy of Education Society,* pp. 100–104. Terre Haute: Indiana State University.

White, C. J., Andino-Demyan, D., Primer, D., & Storz, M. (1996). Constructing a scholarly community of jazz freedom fighters: (Re) writing the university classroom for the postmodern world. *Planning and Changing*. no. 27 (1/2). pp. 58–73

White, C. J., Sakiestewa, N., & Shelley C. (1998). TRIO: The unwritten legacy. *The Journal of Negro Education, 67*, (4), pp. 444–454.

White, C.J., Mogilka, J., & Ford Slack, P.J. (1998). Disturbing the colonial frames of ethnographic representation: Releasing feminist imagination on the academy. In N.K. Denzin (Ed.). *Cultural Studies: A Research Annual*, (3). London: Sage Publications, Inc.

Woodson, C. G. (1992). *The Mis-education of the American negro*. Trenton: Africa World Press.

 *Cultural* **Critique**   *General Editor: Norman K. Denzin*

Cultural Critique is a research monograph series drawing from those scholarly traditions in the social sciences and the humanities that are premised on critical, performance-based cultural studies agenda. Preference is given to experimental, risk-taking
manuscripts that are at the intersection of interpretative theory, critical methodology,
culture, media, history, biography, and social structure. Asserting that culture is best
understood as a gendered performance, this international-research monograph series
combines ethnography and critical textual approaches to the study of popular literature, media, myth, advertising, religion, science, cinema, television, and the new
communication and information technologies. This new series creates a space for the
study of those global cultural practices and forms that shape the meanings of self,
identity, race, ethnicity, class, nationality, and gender in the contemporary world.

Preference will be given to authors who engage a variety of critical qualitative,
interpretive methodologies, from semiotics and critical textual analysis to interpretive
and auto-ethnography, personal narrative, and the practices of investigative, civic,
intimate, and immersion journalism. We seek non-conventional, experimental manuscripts. Qualitative methods are material and interpretive practices. They do not stand
outside politics and cultural criticism. Critical methodologies advance the project of
moral criticism. This spirit, critically imagining and pursuing a more democratic
society, has been a guiding feature of cultural studies from the very beginning. Contributors to the Cultural Critique series will forward this project. They will take up
such methodological and moral issues as the local and global, text and context, voice,
writing for the other, and the author presence in the text. Cultural Critique understands that the discourses of a critical, moral methodology are basic to any effort to re-
engage the promise of the social sciences for democracy in the twenty-first century.
Cultural Critique publishes works of ethnopoetry, auto-ethnography, creative non-
fiction, performance texts, book reviews, and critical analyses of current media repre-
sentations and formations. Projected contents (and contributors) will be drawn from
scholarly traditions in the social sciences and humanities, including history, anthropol-
ogy, sociology, communications, art history, education, American studies, kinesiology,
performance studies, and English. The scope of submissions will be international.

For additional information about this series or for the submission of manuscripts,
please contact:

> Dr. Norman K. Denzin
> University of Illinois, Institute of Communications Research
> 228 Gregory Hall, 810 So. Wright Street
> Urbana, IL 61801

To order other books in this series, please contact our Customer Service Department:

> (800) 770-LANG (within the U.S.)
> (212) 647-7706 (outside the U.S.)
> (212) 647-7707 FAX

or browse online by series:

WWW.PETERLANGUSA.COM